GWLAD! GWLAD?- An Invitation To A Party
by
Aled Gwyn Job
ISBN: 978-1-9165001-2-9

Published by

i2i
PUBLISHING

i2i Publishing
Manchester. UK
www.i2ipublishing.co.uk

"Cyflwynedig i'm Mam a Nhad am ddangos y ffordd imi ei throedio o'r cychwyn cyntaf"

"What man actually needs in life is not some tension-less state, but rather the striving and struggling for some goal worthy of him" Victor Frankel.

<u>Aberystwyth November 17, 2017</u>

I awaken to the sound of the waves crashing on the sea shore outside my window. One of the delights of staying on Aberystwyth's beautiful seaside promenade.

But Autumn, and it's dank and gloomy nature has also accompanied me here to one of my very favourite places in the whole of Wales.

The weather seems to be a perfect metaphor for Wales's current mood and temperature. The EU Referendum of 2016 had completely upended the status quo of many years standing and demolished the usual Welsh political platitudes about the blessings of EU membership. Wales had followed its neighbour England in voting 'Leave' in the referendum.

The country's national party, Plaid Cymru, had unwisely perhaps, decided to adopt a monolithic position of out and out support for the EU, rather than allowing more sceptical views within the party to be aired and discussed. The result seemed to have placed them on the wrong side of history in the most important public vote for generations. All this had left many people here in a complete state of bewilderment and angst.

This confusion was taken to another level entirely over the following year or so, thanks to the rank incompetence of the UK government in failing to define the terms of departure from the EU. Under the strange premiership of Theresa May, the exact nature of the Brexit beast remained as elusive as ever. Uncertainty seemed to be the only certainty in town.

And now, on top of all that, Wales was struggling to come terms with one of the biggest political stories ever to occur here - the suicide of a leading Assembly Member, Welsh Labour's Carl Sargeant at the start of November 2017.

The popular AM, one of the very few working-class members at the Assembly had taken his own life a few days after being removed from First Minister Carwyn Jones's

Cabinet. The AM had lost his post as Cabinet Secretary for Communities and Children following anonymous female complaints concerning his personal conduct. The story, and the related accusations had been splashed all over the Welsh media that weekend. Desperate attempts to find out about the nature of the complaints from his solicitor over the weekend had been met with a wall of silence. On the Monday morning, Carl Sargeant's body was discovered by his wife in their house at Connah's Quay, north-east Wales.

As the story unfolded, a stunned public in Wales had to get up to speed with a horrific story, involving to varying degrees, political manoeuvrings, the growing influence of lobbyists, feminist politics and what was being referred to as a bullying and toxic culture within the National Assembly in Cardiff Bay.

New revelations were being presented almost on a daily basis by a media which could hardly believe their luck in finding such a story amidst the mind-numbing tediousness which usually passed for political life in Wales.

One could almost imagine that the form of devolution that had developed in Wales since 1998 had been designed to make politics here appear to be both incredibly boring and futile. But then former Prime Minister, Tony Blair, the architect of devolution in Scotland and Wales would never impose such a plan. Would he?

The bitter irony was that it had taken a tragic suicide to bring things to life here.

The wider Carl Sargeant story seemed to encapsulate everything that was wrong with modern Wales. A ruling party, Welsh Labour, had reigned supreme for almost 20 years at the National Assembly following another 80 years or so when they had completely monopolised Welsh political life on all levels. Such unchallenged dominance could only lead to both unbridled arrogance and entitlement, and a sense that they could do whatever they liked in power.

With no proper Welsh media to scrutinize them, a divided opposition and a national party struggling ever to reach 20% support in the country- Wales seemed destined to be ruled by Labour forever. A whole nation seemed trapped in some type of unending Kafkaesque nightmare.

Then there was the emergence of a group of influential lobbyists in situ at Cardiff Bay with many of them moving seamlessly from jobs with political parties to the media to lobbying firms and back again: completely under the radar as far as the Welsh public were concerned. A mini-Westminster with its own revolving-door reward culture for a select few had now embedded itself in Wales.

And now a growing culture of anonymous complaints about the behaviour of public figures, where reputations and careers could be trashed overnight by accusations with little or no natural justice in place had ended with a very public suicide and a huge national tragedy.fff

Several months later, the family of Carl Sargeant, frustrated that the official inquest into his death had yet to commence, started a judicial review against the Welsh Labour Government. The official inquest had to be postponed for the judicial review to take place. There were murmurings that the briefings against Carl Sargeant and the accusations made against him could well have been instigated by those who wanted to stop Sergeant from putting his name forward to replace Carwyn Jones as First Minister when he stood down.

Had people in high places in Cardiff Bay cynically made use of a Westminster scandal about a politician placing his hand on the knee of a female journalist to target Carl Sargeant with some equivalent minor actions? It appeared that it wasn't just female lobbyists in Cardiff Bay who were out to get him. It was some of his own Welsh Labour colleagues. The story was getting murkier and murkier.

On this gloomy November day in Aberystwyth, it seemed most timely therefore that a meeting had been called to discuss the formation of a new political party for Wales. The meeting was arranged by the political blogger, Jac o The North (Royston Jones, of Abergynolwyn).

I had long been a follower of Jac's Blog since he seemed to the only one really undertaking any journalistic investigations into the varying problematic elements of modern Welsh life and exposing a litany of corruption and abuses of power linked to one-party rule in Wales. I admired his bloody-minded willingness to say it as it is honestly, without fear or favour.

I had offered to provide a simultaneous translation service at the meeting for a discounted rate - an offer which Royston had gladly accepted. It was also a way to gauge whether this idea of a new party had any legs at all.

Royston cuts a dapper figure, slim with twinkling eyes and his broad Swansea tones undiluted by many years living in Abergynolwyn, near Tywyn in north-west Wales. He will make a habit of turning up to meetings over the next few months in some snappy shades, which make him look seriously cool. His encyclopaedic knowledge of all things Welsh, and an ability to cut through all the bullshit to focus on what's really important is to become a key feature of developments over the next few months.

On arrival at Y Morlan, a community centre run by the Presbyterian Church of Wales in Aberystwyth, I also get to meet the famous Big Gee. Gwilym ab Ioan of Aberaeron, like Royston a veteran of the Welsh nationalist cause. Gwilym with his long trademark white beard bears an uncanny resemblance to someone. I just can't place at the time. A genial man further enhanced by his soft and endearing Ceredigion tones. Genial but formidable.

A formidable intelligence, a formidable drive, and as I was to find out in due course, a formidable temper as well at times.

Some time later, Gwilym sends me a link to a video of his son, Teifion Lewis, an amateur boxer from Carmarthen, in action in the ring. Teifion looks very handy in the ring, ready and willing to take on all challengers. A combative, 'warrior gene' must run in the family as Big Gee himself admits to me later.

Gwilym chairs the meeting and introduces himself as the interim Chairperson. To my discomfort, I'm placed on the stage, next to him and Royston, as though we were part of some triumvirate of officers, already in place for the new party.

It's a bizarre situation. I've never been on the stage before as a Simultaneous Translator in a public meeting. Translators are supposed to merge into the background and be inconspicuous, for goodness stage. What on earth am I doing up here on stage? It's much too close to the action for my liking but having just met Gwilym and sized him up I decided to stay put. I think this is a good call.

Around twenty-five people from various parts of Wales have turned up for the meeting - primarily middle-aged and male. The lack of female input into proceedings was very noticeable and would become a recurrent theme in group discussions over the next few months.

The meeting gets underway, and a guy called Simon Foster Evans from Bridgend gets into his stride at the back, rambling on about the EU. Simon has an odd habit of pacing up and down whilst making his point. Gwilym however has rolled up his sleeves and is in no mood to allow too much of this, and he puts down an early marker by urging Simon to get to his point.

Gwilym and Simon are to have a major falling-out on the internet supporters' forum set up for the new party in due course. This does not surprise me in the slightest having witnessed this initial encounter.

An individual by the name of Gruff Meredith from Cardiff (later to find fame in his own right by becoming the editor of the newly-vamped Y Cymro Welsh-language paper) then pipes up to say that he has already set up a new party called Sovereign Wales. Although he doesn't spell this out as such, it's obvious that Gruff wants this to become the official vehicle for the new party.

It becomes even more confusing when another attendee, Ioan Richard from the Swansea Valley says that he has also got his own party in place, with its own designated logos and emblems registered with the Electoral Commission, which could be transferred to the new entity. You wait an eternity for a new party, and then three arrive all together...

Ioan is another one to test Gwilym's patience to the limit as a Chairperson, since he is even worse than Simon. He takes what seems to be around ten minutes to explain a point that could be made in around two at most. There's a look of quiet despair on many people's faces as Ioan goes on and on.

However, he seems genuine enough in his wish to transfer the registered Welsh dragon and map of Wales to any new party that emerges from the meeting. The beauty of doing this is that it would prevent any other political party from making any use of these emblems - both of which are totemic Welsh emblems.

Everyone agrees that this is a good idea despite Ioan's verbosity. I later discover that Ioan has been a councillor for something like forty years or more. He's had plenty of time to practice his art. Although he doesn't appear in any further meetings, Ioan's transfer of the registration of his original party's name to the Electoral Commission is to cause some major headaches later on in the process.

An older guy from Blaenau Gwent, whose name I didn't catch is next up. He seems very defeatist about the whole idea from the outset, spending most of his time bemoaning the mistakes made by the national movement in the past and more or less predicting that these will be repeated again this time round. And anyway, he doesn't think he's got the time anyway.

I'm not too sure why's he turned up to be honest. Probably just fancied a run to Aberystwyth and back for the day.

Others speak up in their turn, including a couple from Wrecsam in north-east Wales, and a Welsh-speaking Glaswegian called Alan Hughes living near Dolgellau. A young guy called James Llewelyn-Henton from Neath then introduces himself to everyone. James will eventually take the role of the token youngster in the process of getting a new party up and running. He tells us that he's studying intelligence and security at the University in Aberystwyth.

There's a couple of fellows from Pembrokeshire, south-west wales, and a distinguished looking gentleman in the front-row, who seems very clued-up about things. I later discover that this is Gwyn Wigley Evans, from Llanddeiniol just outside Aberystwyth, a former Vice President of the Farmers Union of Wales.

The name is a dead giveaway in Wales, seeing that Dafydd Wigley (now Lord Wigley) used to be a leading light in Plaid Cymru politics, and is a former leader of the party. Gwyn turns out to be a cousin of Lord Wigley - although there doesn't seem to be much love lost between them on Gwyn's part. Maybe that's down to the fact that he actually worked for his cousin in London at one point.

That seems interesting, especially as Dafydd Wigley is regarded almost as royalty here in Wales. Typically, nobody batted an eyelid here when he decided to become a Lord. Even though Plaid Cymru's official policy is to oppose the House of Lords. I make a mental note to ask Gwyn about this in future.

The meeting moves on to discuss the question of a name for the new party. Gruff sees his chance once again and proposes 'Sovereign Wales' as an ideal name. He suggests this would save everyone a lot of time and bother in thinking up a new name. Prophetic words indeed as things would turn out.

A John Davies from Pembrokeshire then suggests the 'Welsh Independence Party'. As I'm up on the stage anyway, I decide to set aside my usual reticence to suggest that maybe the name should be short, snappy and in Welsh.

I do my best, but I find myself rehearsing a well-rehearsed line of mine over the years - I'd be so much better explaining all this on paper - but I'm not completely laughed out of court, so I suppose it is 'mission accomplished' to some extent.

After some debate, Gwilym decides that this issue will be parked over Christmas, in the hope that some form of consensus will be reached by the next meeting in January. The meeting then holds a show of hands to decide whether to proceed with the idea of establishing a new political party for Wales to campaign for Independence. It's an overwhelming Yes.

Gwilym is chosen as interim chairman and Royston as Treasurer. The tag of being 'Gwilym and Jac's Party' is to dog the party over the coming months. Murmurings about a new 'right wing' party are to be disseminated all over Wales over the coming weeks and months.

As a small nation of three million people, things don't get hidden away here for long. The close social interactions between people and communities here means that information and dis-information is relayed up and down this land with lightning speed and regularity. The downside of such immediate transparency is that hearsay, conjecture and rumour can be transposed into hard and immutable facts in a very short space of time.

As such, it suited the detractors and the naysayers to focus on the 'Gwilym and Jac Party' line from the very start. It seemed to be accepted shorthand for the belief that the new party would be a throwback to the past, inhabited by dinosaurs, both by age and beliefs. Those instant pundits seemed confident in their belief that the new party would be very traditional and old-fashioned, promoting a view of Wales which was both regressive and outdated. This 'Gwilym and Jac' saga was eventually come to a head late the following summer.

From my vantage point on the stage that day, it seems to me that the meeting has attracted quite a disparate collection of individuals. United only by an agreed consensus that Wales needs a new political party to push for Independence. But will it be the equivalent of the Judean People's Front? Or the People's Front of Judea?

If this enterprise is ever to get off the ground, these differing individuals will need to develop some form of team ethos over the next few months. I think to myself that Gwilym's really got his work cut out as a kind of self-appointed manager on this outfit.

Sasha Baron Cohen is the brilliant TV satirist who rose to fame with his Ali G character, an inner-city rapper dressed up in a yellow shell suit who somehow managed to interview and embarrass unsuspecting public figures on camera. One of his most hilarious lines in responding to his guests' anger when outrageous questions are put to them, was his, "Is it cos I is Black?"

At the end of this first meeting, I had the thought: "Is it cos I is middle-aged?!"

Where for heaven's sake were all the young people today? Apart from James, everyone else was over their 50s. I am 54. But with the young people of today consumed by technology, and living life as 24/7 consumers above all else, community and political activism to try and change society seem to belong to an age which has long ago faded away, as far as they are concerned.

A generation facing paying back £30,00 to £40,000 after University are also much more likely to be passive, and less interested in engaging in political activity of any sort. The marketization of our society over the past generation has ironically led to less and less real choice of how society is to be run. Thanks Tony Blair. Some legacy you have.

If the youngsters of today are so passive, maybe the mantle of protest and activism has indeed fallen upon middle aged/older people? But what is it about reaching middle-age that makes people of this sort believe they can change things? Is it a mid-life thing? Is it a mortality thing? Is it a man thing even??

It's an issue I'll keep returning to time and time again over the next few months.

We soon find out that the accusations of being 'old-fashioned' and 'out-dated' are to be proved completely wrong in at least one crucial area: the use of the internet and social media to promote the new party. This was to prove a key component of the work from the outset. It soon became obvious to me that Big Gee had been thinking about and planning this operation for some time.

I finally remember now who he resembles - Gandolf of Lord of the Rings! For someone who is so clueless about popular culture usually, I'm quite pleased with myself that I've managed to dredge that up. An image of Gandolf's wizardry somehow seems apt in view of the way that Gwilym's expertise as an engineer and IT specialist was put to work in devising a number of websites, for potential supporters of the new party.

With a gap of two months between the first two meetings, it quickly became apparent how important a tool this was to be to allow the attendees and registered supporters to strike up a connection with each other from the start, to swap ideas and thoughts and create some form of momentum for the fledgling new party.

PEN PORTRAIT 1:

Royston Jones.
Born in Swansea. Living in Abergynolwyn, Gwynedd.

I've been involved in politics since the heady days of the mid-1960s when it seemed Wales was finally waking up to our abusive and exploitive relationship with England. The '60s passed and with it the optimism, as too many fell into the trap of believing that the best way to protect Wales from London's negligence or hostility, especially when the Tories were in power, was to vote for the Labour Party.

Yet on it went, Labour maintaining its dominance in Wales by blaming the Tories for everything that was wrong with Wales - even when there was a Labour government in Westminster! In this bipolar political universe, Plaid Cymru - certainly from the 1980s onwards - surrendered to the gravitational pull of the Labour Party. 'Fellow socialists, innit'.

As someone who had always wanted independence I did not welcome devolution. I suppose I went along with it in the hope that it might be the first step on the road to independence. How wrong I was.

Not only are we further from independence than we were in 1999, but Wales is also poorer than it was before devolution. We are less healthy, and our children get a poorer education than their counterparts in England, Scotland and Northern Ireland.

Under devolution Wales has gone backwards! How could this happen?

It could and has happened because for 20 years Wales has been managed by a political party that cares nothing for Wales beyond delivering up as many Labour MPs as possible for Westminster and stopping any other party controlling the Cynulliad.

Yet real power lies with civil servants answering to London who have allowed successive Labour 'governments' down Cardiff docks, to use Wales as a testing ground for legislation, dole out vast sums to its client class in our bloated third sector, and turn people off politics generally and devolution in particular.

But they overplayed their hand.

The decline of Wales, both relative to other countries and to our own past, is now so obvious that there is no disguising it. It affects too many people, to the point where across the land, apathy is being replaced with palpable anger.

Anyone looking around Wales today can see countless issues needing to be tackled; yet we had no political party prepared to face up to the problems, let alone come up with answers. Which is why we needed a new party.

A political party that rejects over·development in one city, managed decline in other urban areas, and large tracts of our countryside being relegated to 'tourist destination' status. A party that believes all areas of Wales must be treated fairly, prosperity must be shared equally, and Welsh identity must be defended.

Wales is now at rock bottom, and the only way is up. And I say that because after twenty years of Labour managing Wales on behalf of London, we are poorer, less healthy, and less well educated, both relative to neighbouring countries and to Wales of the recent past. Fewer and fewer people now believe Labour when they attribute this decline to Tories or sunspots, or to dismiss it as propaganda put out by 'malcontents' like me. People no longer buy such nonsense because they can see the decline all around them.

From now on the Welsh national interest must take priority over everything. And the national interest can only be served with independence.

December 9th 2017

By this point over 100 people had registered on the website set up by Big Gee as registered supporters. This was no mean feat, bearing in mind that everything was still so sketchy and there were no clear definitions in mind as to the general direction of the new entity.

Although I had shied away from being on the initial Steering Committee of nine people, Gwilym phones me up before Christmas to ask me whether I could do him a favour and input the names of all those who had signed up as registered supporters into a spread-sheet he has prepared. And to write back to these new supporters to thank them and acknowledge their interest.

He obviously knows little about my organizational capacities at this point. My secretarial duties quietly fade away early in the new year as it dawns upon Gwilym that he'd be better off doing all this himself. Although he was practically doing everything else as well, at this stage. He was and would remain the driving force behind the new party.

December 17th 2017

I travel down to Cardiff for the annual office Christmas bash. As a translator for the Presbyterian Church of Wales, I work out of an office in Caernarfon, so I don't see my office workmates all that often. It's a good opportunity to touch base with everyone.

This time, it was held in the lavish surroundings of Cardiff Castle, along with harp recitals and traditional carol singing. The girls in the office were in party mood, and really going for it with wine, song and seemingly never-ending group selfies keeping them royally entertained. Who said Presbyterians can't have fun?!

Thankfully for a notorious party-pooper such as myself, I was situated on a quieter adjacent table. I was placed next to our General Secretary, Rev Meirion Morris, an university contemporary of mine, who has worked his way up within the organization to take on the main role in our denomination.

Fair play to Meirion, he's had his own struggles with his mental health over the years, but you could not wish for a more dedicated and conscientious General Secretary. I pull his leg about the title sometimes, bearing in mind that the most famous general secretary post of course was reserved for the leader of the Communist Party in the Soviet Union.

I suggest to Meirion that the communist grass-roots would have been easier to handle than some Christians in modern Wales, with their attachment to church buildings above everything else and a general reluctance to engage in the type of changes so sorely needed today. But of course, with no gulags in Wales to place such backsliders, it does make things slightly more difficult for him.

Meirion mentions his recent visit to Northern Ireland, where apparently there are 250,000 members in the Presbyterian Church of Ireland, compared to the paltry 18,000 members we have in the Presbyterian Church of Wales. Meirion marvels at a society where faith is still a central part of people's lives, congregations of a 100 + every Sunday a regular occurrence in all their churches and young people still a key part of their congregations. Compared to modern-day Wales, with its dwindling church attendance and congregations invariably 60+, Northern Ireland must seem to be some form of a Presbyterian utopia. No wonder Meirion is so taken with the place.

It's quite ironic that the political manifestation of the Presbyterian Church of Ireland is mainly the Democratic Unionist Party(DUP) - currently holding up the Conservative Government at Westminster. The DUP are perhaps lampooned too easily about their genuinely held opposition to gay marriage and abortion and so on. Although perhaps their belief in the earth being less than 6,000 years old does deserve to be ridiculed. But it does seem ironic that they have an unwavering loyalty to a Britain which by now holds such diametrically opposed views to the DUP on all matters of personal morality.

I don't follow these points up with Meirion so as not to spoil the Christmas spirit. It's an enjoyable evening, but I'm perfectly happy to call it a day around 11.00 and head off back to my hotel in the city centre.

Christmas Day and Boxing Day, December 25/26

Once again, I'm indebted to the generosity and conviviality of my sister Angharad to spend the two days with the family at Llanfairpwll. Every single middle-aged man should have a sister like Angharad!

We all have a great time together as a family. My sister and I count our blessings that our parents, though in their early eighties are in good health, and that we live so close to each other.

But I'm also looking forward to a walking break arranged by my mate Big D from Aberystwyth, just after Christmas. Big D and I walked Offa's Dyke together last summer, which was a fantastic experience all round. Well, let's be perfectly honest here - Big D walked the entire length over a fortnight, and I completed a mere third of the course. But it was a really important event for me at that time in my life, and I will always be thankful to him for arranging that journey.

This time Big D had organized a two day walk for us in the Peak District, with accommodation booked at the YHA Harlington Hall. Allegedly this was where Bonny Prince Charlie (Charles Edward Stuart) stayed overnight on his way down to challenge for the English Crown in 1745. Charlie and his army reached Derby only to turn back. The likelihood is that he could have gone all the way to London such was the weakness of the forces ranged against him at that point. His retreat from Derby was the end of his hopes to regain the

Crown for the Stuarts. Scotland and its increasingly strained relationship with Westminster was to be a regular feature over the months to come.

We reach Harlington Hall in the early evening to find a comfortable and warm environment awaiting us. As two middle-aged men we need to feel no embarrassment in seeking accommodation in such a youth hostel, since most of the other guests are also around our age as well. As the old saying goes, "youth is wasted on the young".

The Peak District does not disappoint. The undulating hills we explore remind me of Dyffryn Clwyd in Denbighshire, north-east Wales, and the people are so friendly and down to earth here, always willing to strike up a conversation. The small, close-knit rural communities we encounter and their adaptability to a life on not much money are somehow, a further reminder of Wales.

Big D's got a real ability to relate to people. He's has a very warm personality. But I'm always taking the mick out of his accent when he speaks English. It's just a weird combination of Cardiff, Scouse and Manc. He blames the Manc on the year he spent there doing an MA in Screenwriting. He's not sure where the Scouse element has crept in. And the Cardiff?

"Ceeediiiiff – well what do you expect after nearly 30 years in the big smoke mate"? he asks, as if that has been some form of life sentence for him.

Heavy snowfall over night adds to the whole magical experience. I spend half an hour after breakfast just watching the snow fall outside the lounge bay window of Harlington Hall. The peace and silence that the falling snow seems to evoke is indescribable.

Big D and I set off for a 20-mile hike through a snow-covered landscape, finished off with a scrumptious late lunch at a local pub. Is there anything better than getting up of a morning and knowing that you are going to walk 10, 15, 20 miles that day?

There's something almost akin to a spiritual experience in motion when you go on a long walk with a close friend in nature. The very act of walking together in the open air encourages an openness and frankness to talk and share about life in a way that is seldom found in other day-to-day circumstances.

Men are notorious for not really talking to each other. That's definitely not the case with Big D and Me. Is it the walking? Or is it the fact that we are two single, middle-aged men who have a deep need for meaningful friendship and connection in our lives?

My friendship with Big D is probably the closest friendship I have in my life. There's nothing I like better than chewing the cud with him talking about the things that really matter to the both of us.

We have a great time together over the three days and agree that Wales needs to become a walking nation where regular walking becomes a feature of everyday life for all. I remember reading somewhere that our ancestors on the African Savannah would probably walk around 8-10 miles a day in search of food.

Walking is just wired into our very DNA. Our bodies crave it, just as much as they crave water, food and air. It is quite literally the best therapy available. I just couldn't live without walking every day now.

Big D's got a dream about a nationwide walking trail which could serve to unite north and south Wales. As he says, all the traffic goes southwards at present, with so many people from the north travelling down to Cardiff for the rugby and soccer games. But there doesn't seem to be the same volume of traffic the other way.

"We've got to get rid of this northophobia somehow - and maybe a walking trail would encourage more people from the south to explore the north and encourage more of a national conversation between us," he says. He's got some good ideas has Big D.

Six months later, I hear about the "Rhiannon Trail"- Big D's idea is taking form in the shape of a proposal submitted to the Welsh Government by an individual by the name of Neil Anderson. A 300 km walking and cycling upland route to unite north and south along the spine of Wales at a cost of some £60 million.

He says the route could lead to employment opportunities in new accommodation, eating facilities and cycle repair outlets along the route, and a range of associated work opportunities in interests such as photography, ornithology, cycle repair and so forth. I think it's a great idea. Let's hope the politicians can get behind it.

As we travel back to Wales, the heavy snow in the Peak District disappears gradually, and I eventually arrive home to find that the key from my dorm at the Youth Hostel had somehow fallen into my rucksack. How the hell did that happen?!

I get an intensely irate message from Big D on my phone within minutes expressing his huge displeasure: "Anarchist by name, anarchist by nature!!!" he writes accusingly.

That's a bit unfair on the anarchists I feel. I don't remember any anarchist thinker suggesting that supporters try to undermine organisations such as the YHA by depriving them of their keys. But D is absolutely right to take me to task on this one. There'll be no further contact until the key is returned to Harlington Hall!

How on earth am I going to cope with that?! I usually text Big D around six times a day at least...

It's like being plugged into a second brain I guess. I'll just have to get on with one brain I suppose.But, that's what I like about Big D. He will tell you his mind straight. Everyone needs a Big D in their life.

PEN PORTRAIT 2:

Gwilym Ab Ioan.
Born in Trefenter. Now living in Aberaeron

I was born in 1954 in Banc Llyn a mountain homestead near Llyn Eiddwen in Trefenter on Mynydd Bach. A desolate area on the highland moorlands of Ceredigion. I can trace my family ancestors on my father's side back ten generations by oral tradition. They were all born in a semi-crofter 'tyddyn' called Llocau Bach on the Lledrod side of the mountain. My family history goes back to the period of the early 1800's and beyond, when they were instrumental in 'Rhyfel Y Sais Bach'.

I grew up with the patriotic hearth-side stories of Rhyfel Y Sais Bach, and much more. With the resentment of the injustices suffered by my family and their neighbours in the community as clear as crystal in my mind as a child and later as an adult. I grew up yearning for freedom from England and vowed at a very early age, to do my part in repossessing our colonised country and handing it back to my people.

After studying Physics, English and Maths at Tregaron County School, I went to the University of Wales Institute of Science and Technology in Cardiff, graduating as an electronics engineer in 1975.

Many years later, after the death of my first wife, I returned to Ceredigion from south Wales, and I now live in Aberaeron. It was during this period that I started in earnest to become politically active and involved once more. In a very short time I became the chair of my local branch, then the chair of Plaid Cymru Ceredigion. From there I became one of the vice presidents of Plaid Cymru.

In 2002 I resigned from Plaid, following their failure to support me on a public statement I made reflecting my views – that I uphold to this day. Simply put, their cowardice, and lack of integrity to tell the truth, instead displaying a hypocritical face to the public, forced me to turn my back on them in utter disgust.

Those views I made public drew attention to Wales becoming a replica of Montana in the US (that feels the pressure of drop-outs from urban areas from other States). We suffer from the same phenomenon, of becoming the dumping ground for 'oddballs, social misfits and society drop-outs from the English cities'. I believe that my statement has been vindicated many times over in later years. It is becoming ever more evident that the situation has worsened and is becoming common knowledge to a wider circle in Wales.

Overall this trend is promoted by the Councils across many areas of Wales and the Third Sector fuelled by the Labour government in Y Senedd, who give financial incentives to encourage this process of cloaked colonisation, resulting in the demise of our nation, it's language, history, culture and heritage, as our country becomes further assimilated into England by sheer force of numbers – put crudely · we are facing the cultural genocide of a nation by stealth.

It would be utterly stupid to suggest that this is the case with all people from England who settle in our country. There are those who are fair and just-minded, who willingly assimilate into our country's communities, support our struggles and contribute to our economy (as many leading lights and fervent workers in nationalist organisations have in the past). They, more often than not, make genuine efforts to learn our language and learn about our history and culture, and by extension realizing and sympathising with our plight. I would welcome with open arms · such good, honest and genuine people, in any numbers. My second wife is English and hails from Merseyside.

Following my resignation from Plaid Cymru, due to what I still believe to be cowardice and a losing of the way from their original objectives from when they were first formed, I became involved with the Independent Wales Party. Unfortunately that was short-lived, basically because of a lack of planning, management and an urge to run before they could walk. Sadly they failed and disappeared.

Fifteen years later (after a self-imposed period of exile in the political wilderness) I was invited by an old friend of mine – Royston Jones - to construct and host his blog site - 'jacothenorth', which has become phenomenally popular, thanks to the fantastic investigative journalism that Royston is involved in. His blog site became a catalyst for likeminded people who viewed the general situation in Wales in the same way as I do. Gradually this collection of likeminded people, grew organically to the point where the call for a new party became very loud. Consequently, a public meeting, which I was asked to chair, was arranged at Aberystwyth in November **2017**. The large gathering voted unanimously to form a party, with the sole intention of accomplishing full independent sovereignty for our country. A Steering Committee was formed at the end of the meeting, and those involved set about the task of laying the foundation for our new party.

We also have social media outlets, and a private supporters web-site and a supporters' Forum for open discussions amongst our supporters. Everything we do involves our supporters. Our policies will include suggestions from all citizens, and we have no pre-set doctrines, dogmas or ideology: we will only proceed with policies that are directly beneficial to Wales and her citizens and their welfare. Our major goal is independence to carry our country forward to the best of its abilities.

We believe that where we have gone wrong in the past, is by creating parties that were no different to the old established parties in their approach and set-up, just a different flavour. They used a system that has its roots in the 19th century and which is by now defunct, not only defunct, but one that people have turned their backs on. Even the way we chose our name was a break from convention. All our supporters were invited to put forward names and an on-line poll was conducted to find the most popular. Over seventy names were proposed and Ein Gwlad was the chosen one.

It has been agreed that we will be a syncretic party, formed on modern lines, and using the same concepts and techniques as the other hugely popular and successful syncretic parties that are springing up across Europe. Ein Gwlad will be the first syncretic party in Wales and will lead the charge in this exciting new era of people-centred politics.

Like someone who has searched their whole life in pursuit of the right religion, I feel that at last I've found my true home, with a party whose ethos is truth, openness, a loathing of political correctness and control by elitists and empirical forces. Ein Gwlad has arrived to wash away those things that have kept us captive for so long.

January 2nd 2018

The web forums set up by Gwilym are hotting up. A number of regular contributors are starting to appear, and some interesting ideas are being circulated. One key issue is the need to consider some media publicity for the ideas, without giving too much away at the start. Although it wasn't specifically outlined in the first meeting, I get the impression that this will be a 'slowly, slowly, catchy monkey' type of operation. Indeed several months would elapse before the new party was to be presented to the public.

By this point, I was starting to consider how I could help out practically. Although my original intention was to take a back-seat, I was starting to warm to the idea of the enterprise, despite the momentous task that lay ahead. I suppose I've always been an idealist in life. You don't survive life as the son of a Minister in Wales without some ideals permeating your very soul as an individual.

The availability of the web-based forums and the opportunity to swap ideas with like-minded individuals embarking on a journey together were starting to persuade me. With walking having become such a central feature of my life over the past two years, this venture seemed to be an extension of that principle somehow. But this was sure going to be a long trek.

I had no desire whatever to become a future candidate for any party that emerged and to become a politician. I am of course completely unsuited for such an undertaking anyway because of my temperament. I'm just too emotional. Too passionate. Tears come too easily for me. But I was also beginning to sense that the very idea of a politician, in the traditional way of thinking of politicians, was by now fast becoming obsolete and discredited.

One could perhaps track this overwhelming distaste for politicians back to PM Tony Blair's decision to take the UK to war on a false premise in 2003. A million people had marched through London that summer against the idea of attacking Iraq, but we were still dragged into a war by the warmonger politicians in Westminster. The disastrous results of that war in terms of 500,000 Iraqi lives lost and the growth of terrorism throughout the Middle East ever since, had been a hammer blow for the public's trust in politicians.

A couple of tepid enquiries into that war further eroded people's faith in the political process. This was followed in turn by the Westminster Expenses Scandal of 2009 and the Austerity Agenda imposed since 2010. And now we had the continuing car-wreck that was Brexit where the politicians concerned were seeking to out-do each other in sheer incompetence and hubris.

I've always been intrigued by the personal vanity which persuades an individual that they as one person, can conceivably represent the interests of 50,000 to 70,000 (average constituency size of a Parliamentary seat). It seems to me to be a completely ridiculous and archaic concept. The concept of representative democracy has run its course. The fact that the Westminster fallacy was now being replicated now here in Wales just made it worse somehow.

Surely, in 2018 a more collaborative, co-operative and citizen-focused political approach was sorely needed. i.e. a true participative democracy. As much as I am a committed Welsh nationalist, I'm also just as committed to seeing interactive democracy introduced into our every-day lives, where people can have a real say in how their communities and working lives are organized. It's the Anarchist in me I suppose, misplaced keys and all.

So what could I do exactly? Well, I suppose I can write. My training as a journalist and a translator had provided plenty of experience in that direction. As someone who readily acknowledges myself as an introvert, I've always found that writing is the best vehicle to express myself in life. I've always found great wisdom in the quote: "How do I know what I think until I see what I write?"

One medium that could be used for this purpose was nation.cymru, a new Welsh news site, set by Journalist lecturer Ifan Morgan Jones on a voluntary basis back in May 2017. It quickly developed a keen following in Wales, being the 'go-to' place on the net for many news junkies in Wales - who are so meagrely served by the conventional media here.

The emergence of the web-site and the huge interest in it seemed to me to be a further indication that Brexit had galvanized the nation in a way that had not happened for many, many years. A number of different articles about Wales and future possibilities for Wales post-Brexit appeared in quick succession, quite often accompanied by a number of comments by different posters. The comments were often a means to develop the original article in new and different directions, and a new, vibrant on-line democracy was starting to emerge.

But, for some reason, Ifan Morgan Jones was later to delete the original comments section after the site went down for a number of days. The site then re-appeared making use of a Facebook application - which was to reduce the number of comments by 80%. Those commentators who had really brought the site alive, just didn't want to be associated with Facebook - the company which found itself mired in a data-tapping scandal in the spring of 2018 - and they just fell away. It seemed a huge own goal and a crying shame.

Although I had no idea that a new party was in the offing at the time, I was fortunate enough to be able to publish an article on nation entitled, 'The Five C's on the Road To Independence', in September 2017.

In it, I had argued that any successful Welsh Independence campaign had to be a broad church, since Wales itself was such a broad church: Welsh-speaking and English-speaking, rural and urban, large cities and small villages, secular and faith-based etc, etc.

I suggested that 5'C's could be targeted:

Cultural Nationalists: these would be those people who identified themselves as Welsh first and foremost. This cut across language barriers, since this could include strongly Welsh-speaking areas like Arfon in the north-west and overwhelmingly English-speaking communities in key areas such as the valleys (where 40% of the Welsh population live).

Collectivists: these would be the people who had traditionally been supportive of the Labour movement and the desire to improve the material conditions of individuals and communities here in Wales

Conservatives: The name 'Conservative' has often been used as a bogeyman by both Labour and Plaid Cymru, but the truth is that there are large swathes of rural Wales where traditional conservative values such as self-responsibility, prudence and enterprise are still very much prized, under a 'small c' mantle perhaps.

Conservationists: A growing section in Wales - people who are concerned about the environment and looking after the landscape. With a love for the land being a key motif for nationalists, this was another key audience that could be targeted.

Cosmopolitans: Over the past few year, Wales has become more cosmopolitan not only in the big cities of Cardiff and Newport, but also in places such as Bangor and Wrexham in the north. Such people could be attracted to the idea of an Independent Wales, free to chart its own course in the world, as 200+ nations have indeed done since 1945.

I finish with a bit of a flourish. As you do.

"I dare say there is a spiritual longing here in Wales for a more cohesive and equal and more people-centred country, free from the venal, money-orientated and class-riven Westminster model which has long lost all its integrity".

This writing thing is starting to take off and I start two blogs in both Welsh and English: www.aledgwyn.co.uk www.Cymro2020.co.uk

Being my usual disorganized self, I find it difficult to post them on the web. Big D, fair play to him, has forgotten about the YHA debacle, and he agrees to post them via his twitter account. Publishing these blogs, with a number of them also appearing on the Welsh language news site, Golwg 360 as well as nation.cymru gives me a boost in confidence and an impetus to keep on writing.

At 54, I find that nothing else in life seems to give me as much pleasure and purpose as writing. "The purpose of life is a life of purpose" as someone once said. Indeed, but why wait 54 years to find that out?!

Writing truly seems to be able to spark off places in my brain which can appear dormant in everyday life, which I can find to be hard work a lot of the time. Why can't life be lived through writing I think to myself? But then where would one find the material to write but from life itself. Writing and Living I realize have to be conjoined together like Siamese twins.

January 6th 2018

I'm unable to make it to the second meeting at the Morlan in January in my new role as interim secretary. I've just had a busy week at Coleg Trefeca, near Brecon in Powys on a new leaders' course with the Presbyterian Church of Wales. I've been following this course for a year.

To be honest, I had become thoroughly fed-up with my translating duties chained to a computer each day and needed a new challenge in my life. Having also learnt more about the mental health perils of heavy computer use, I welcomed the opportunity to get involved with something which meant more interaction with people every day. I had been placed with Seilo Church in Caernarfon, and the new leaders' course was a further part of that work.

I'm lucky to be mentored by Rev Harri Parri, a legendary figure in Caernarfon having been a minister in the town for over 50 years. What I like about Harri is that he's got just as much heart for people outside the church as the ones inside. And he's got a great sense of humour as well.

At one point he had quite a heavy fall in his garden and he then sported a really bad, black eye. When he walks down to the centre of Caernarfon for his daily paper, he meets one of the local characters.

"Oh, Harri Parri (everyone calls him Harri Parri in Caernarfon), what's happened to you?" says this man with concern.

"Oh, I've been fighting," quips Harri.

"Oh, Harri Parri, you shouldn't be fighting at your age you know," comes the shocked response.

I love working in Caernarfon, the capital of Welsh-speaking Wales, with 86% speaking Welsh in the town. There's something very special about this place. There's an earthiness, a vitality and humour about the people here. There's not a lot of money here in general, but there's a huge sense of place, of belonging and identity. And at the heart of that, is the strength of the language which is just a huge bond between people here - it's almost feels like being part of one huge extended family to be working here.

Of course there are social divisions in the town, and some people here are earning sums of money which would be beyond the wildest expectations of the majority, but the shared language seems to transcend those divisions somehow.

I find it interesting to compare Caernarfon to nearby Bangor, only nine miles away. Bangor is the home of the University and a large hospital, and it's Welsh-speaking population is much less than Caernarfon at around 50%. There's not the same kind of community coherence to be seen in Bangor - and perhaps that indeed is fuelled by that lower percentage of Welsh speakers there.

I don't mention my new political interest to my colleagues on the course. As a denomination, the Presbyterian Church of Wales has always been a very conservative institution and generally quite suspicious of any overt political involvement as such. I'm not sure how they would respond to my involvement in this new political initiative to be honest.

Politics, after all, can be confrontational. It is, more often than not, an ego-driven, cynical and Machiavellian world. The complete opposite of what a faith-filled life should aim to be. I suppose.

Can faith and politics ever mix at all? I'm not sure to be honest. It's a tension I have to live with over the next months.

January 20th 2018

More stories are emerging from the Carl Sergeant tragedy. It appears that the lobbying firms in Cardiff Bay were unhappy with Carl Sargeant's unwillingness to provide them with the political access that they were used to gain from other ministers.

Were the lobbying firms (predominantly staffed by females) involved in any way with the sexual allegations that were levelled towards the late AM? Different theories were circulating like wildfire. I found that the name Neil McEvoy kept cropping up in different accounts.

McEvoy was a Plaid Cymru AM, elected to the Assembly in 2016 on the Assembly List system. He was very different to the usual sedate and middle-class politicians that represent Plaid Cymru. Mc'Evoy, a former Labour councillor was abrasive and a maverick they said.

Some months previously, McEvoy had been suspended from the Plaid Cymru group on various charges associated with 'bullying', a term which had now seemingly morphed from the lives of children into the lives of adults in a fairly short period of time. McEvoy was also a very vocal critic of the lobbying industry in Cardiff Bay.

I actually met Neil McEvoy in person some months previously, at a quiz night arranged by Plaid Cymru at their annual conference in Caernarfon. I was there with a friend, and there seemed to be a feverish, "Will he or won't he turn up," kind of atmosphere in the event arranged at Clwb Canol Dre that particular night. McEvoy had just been suspended from the Plaid Cymru group at this point. But, if anything, this had just served to increase his profile. Everyone knew that he would not take this lying down.

The quiz at Clwb Canol Dre starts. Twenty minutes pass, and everyone seems to have relaxed. He's not coming after all.

Suddenly, the door bursts open in a scene that any Western would be proud of. Neil McEvoy swans in adorned in his trademark Cardiff City top, accompanied by what seem to be a set of burly minders. The tension is palpable. People carefully scan their quiz sheets to avoid eye contact or lose themselves in the bottom of their pint glasses.

The only space available in the whole room is next to my friend Aled Vaughan, and we are seated at the back, so Neil McEvoy and his gang squeeze in beside us and join in with the quiz. I immediately find Neil to be a friendly and down-to-earth bloke. Somehow or other, the conversation gets around to George Thomas, the Secretary of Wales in the 60ies - who had a reputation for liking young boys. More evidence of this had recently come to light and a charity in Cardiff had just decided to disassociate themselves from his name , which had previously adorned their building.

Neil tells me that George Thomas used to come along to his boys' soccer club in Cardiff, and he can remember being bounced up and down on his knee on one occasion. Somehow, I can't see Neil being bounced into any situation against his will. But, I venture to say that it was a lucky escape for him. He winces. I later find out that he did actually know some people who were unlucky enough to find themselves the subject of Thomas's 'affections'.

Neil's minders turn out to be members of the Plaid Cymru branch in Plas Marl, one of the most deprived part of Cardiff. They are cracking lads, who tell me that this is the very first time they have ever been up to north wales. These are guys in their forties for heaven's sake!

They say they have been amazed by the scenery they have seen on their journey from Cardiff up to Caernarfon. They had no idea Wales was such a beautiful country they say. I get the impression that these would go through hell and high water for 'Mr Mack'.

Neil hands me a leaflet publicizing a talk he is giving at the town's Celtic Hotel the following morning. This is timed to coincide with the opening of Plaid Cymru's conference; suspended but certainly not silenced!

The room at the Celtic Hotel is packed out the following morning with around one hundred and fifty people present to hear his presentation about a vision of a 'Sovereign Wales'. He's got three headers to his talk:

The individual to be sovereign

The community to be sovereign and

The nation itself to be sovereign.

It's a decent speech and the people there respond well to him. He's not going quietly is he, whispers someone to me as I leave the meeting.

But this spirited meeting seems to mark the high watermark of Neil McEvoy's one-man crusade to reform Plaid Cymru.

Six months later I attend another meeting at the same venue, with McEvoy now having launched his own official 'Propel' movement within Plaid Cymru. A kind of equivalent movement to the role played by 'Momentum' within the Labour Party, with the intention of forcing radical change within the party. Somehow, members are expected to pay a Plaid Cymru membership fee, and another fee to join Propel as well. It seems a big ask.

A paltry thirteen people are in attendance this time (including two members of Fathers for Justice, who have travelled all the way from Shrewsbury for the event). Neil does his best, but he looks completely deflated. I chat again to him at the bar at the end of the meeting. Once again, I'm struck by the complete lack of affectation to the man, and his listening and engaging skills. No wonder he's so good as a campaigning politician on the streets of Cardiff.

There's absolutely none of this, "I'm better and more important than you," element which seems to have afflicted so many of Plaid Cymru's politicians over the years unfortunately. But having spent a good hour previously explaining how he could reform Plaid Cymru from within, Neil then spends an hour and a half demolishing his colleagues in the Bay.

He's brutally honest about them, saying that the ten strong group like the trappings of power that devolution has given them personally, and they have no real desire to rock the boat and really campaign for independence.

"They don't believe in Independence," he claims. "Why would they? They are on a cushy £60-70,000 salary plus expenses, so they don't want anything to put that at risk. They've just gone 'Assembly Native'."

He goes on to say that his fellow Plaid AM's are more interested in cosying up to Labour politicians for some crumbs of individual power and influence, and that their modus operandi for achieving this is mainly to socialize with them in the bars and cafes of Cardiff Bay to achieve this aim.

"*How has the Welsh national cause come to this*?" he asks despairingly.

It's a devastating critique and fits in perfectly with the narrative that the new party has been starting to develop; i.e. that Plaid Cymru have lost their way and that post-Brexit, Wales needs a completely new start.

January 27th 2018

I travel down again to Cardiff, this time to take my daughter, Tesni Haf down to an open day at Cardiff University. She wants to study sociology at the University this coming September. I'm very impressed with the presentations and the opportunities outlined by the course tutors. There's even an option to study abroad for one semester.

I've no worries at all about Tesni leaving home and moving to Cardiff to live. She's mature for her age and a very sociable individual - a very different personality to her Dad, a self-confessed introvert who enjoys spending a lot of time in his own company. I'm so glad that she finds socializing so easy after all my struggles in this department over the years.

But, having read a few interesting books about this recently, I'm starting to become more comfortable about my introversion, even starting to brand myself as a social introvert -

someone who is an introvert by nature but who also enjoys spending time with other people on a regular basis. I'm learning how introverts can be the very best at observing people and events around them and able to write analytically and incisively about what they observe. That could prove handy in my new self-defined role I suppose.

Tesni warns me not to show her up by asking a question as I did at a previous presentation some months ago. I thought it was a half-decent question, but she was dying inside as I spoke apparently. I sometimes forget the cringe factor that parents can present to their teenagers in front of other people, especially their peers.

Despite the impressive presentations put on by the Sociology Department - I can't help feeling that the University want to micro-manage Tesni's future academic experience. A huge amount of emphasis is placed on students using their time to network, to undertake voluntary work and generally avail themselves of every opportunity to promote themselves. It's so different to my own University experience a generation ago, where students such as myself were to all intents and purpose left to their own devices.

There was no pressure at all then to start to build up a CV and market ourselves to anyone as such. But with more students now at University, and those students (and parents) having to pay for it - it seems unavoidable that it's now been consumed by a world of marketing. Does that relentless self-promoting allow any time for political activism, and dreams about changing the world, I ask myself? What a stupid question.

But then, self-marketing is very much the name of the game for these young people. It's almost as natural as breathing itself for them today. So it is such an imposition in a way?

We travel back from Cardiff having had a very enjoyable day together. I have to put up with a constant stream of Abba songs from their greatest hits CD, but I don't complain too much. After all these are precious moments with a daughter who will soon be making her own way in the world. And I've got a soft spot for some of Abba's songs as well. Not that I'd admit that to Tesni of course!

The father-daughter bond is always a close one. Maybe in our case it's even stronger since her mother and I split up when Tesni was very young. It was not an ideal situation by any means but having a direct one-to-one relationship with her from the very start, has perhaps led to a deeper connection and understanding between us than would have been the case in a conventional marriage.

Travelling together in a car is maybe the best way for an adult to communicate with a teenager. I find, that sense of travelling together through space and time and perhaps the lack of direct face-to-face interaction, allows young people to share more and be more forthcoming than in other settings.

After the visit, Tesni finally decides that Cardiff is her first choice. I'm pleased to hear that because Liverpool had also been an option for her. I'm glad she will be staying in Wales. There's more chance of her remaining in Wales to pursue a career if she studies here.

She sets herself a vision of a new life, new opportunities and experiences in Cardiff in September and proceeds to bring that vision into reality by the hard work she puts in over the next few months. In August she eventually achieves the A level grades required by Cardiff University. She'll be going to the Big Smoke!

PEN PORTRAIT No 3

Gwyn Wigley Evans:
Born in Bro Ddyfi. Living in LLanddeiniol, near Aberystwyth

I Joined Plaid Cymru at school at the age of 13. I went on to become the secretary of the London branch for 10 years and became a member of the Hydro group within Plaid Cymru to counter the arguments being presented by the 'loony left'. At the conference in Caergybi in 1983, Dafydd Wigley asked Dafydd Iwan to give a speech demanding that the Hydro group leave the party, which I did. Before this, I and some others had been voluntarily helping Dafydd Wigley MP in London - two of us actually persuaded him to stand against Dafydd Ellis Thomas and win the party leadership.

I got involved in many other things, but not political until a year ago when we first formed Ein Gwlad. I had kept an eye on things along the way and developed ideas not only in Wales but from observations during my extensive travelling and international contacts.

During this time I had nowhere to go, Plaid being the only option for anything close to my aspirations. During my time in London, I lived near Kilburn and I would vote for Sinn Fein!

This, with my working in Catalan showed me there was not only a need for another independence focused party, but there was a ready-made gap there for disaffected, dejected and banned Plaid members. In fact, I had not left Plaid, Plaid had left me, especially with the election of Leanne Wood and her gang who saw the pinnacle of their political life being the take-over of Plaid, not of Wales, rainbow politics and the like. I also had an eye on those voters who do not vote for Plaid Cymru. Plaid has about 20% of the vote. With only around 50% of the electorate voting in Welsh Elections, that means that Plaid have around 10% of the electorate, leaving 90% available.

February 6th 2018

The saga of choosing a name for the new political entity rumbles on. A brilliant exercise in democratizing the processes from the very start or a bewildering waste of time and energy? That all depends on your perspective I suppose.

Big Gee draws up a set of guidelines for the registered supporters to follow and they are invited to take part in an on-line poll to choose the name. The process seems to initiate a fair amount of interest amongst the fifty-three regular posters, although one poster called Westonian, points to inconsistencies in the whole process.

He then ventures that a 'string-pulling cabal' is manipulating the whole exercise from the very start He is duly shot down by Big Gee, who points to the fact that it is a completely open process with everyone equally involved. Westonian, whoever he or she is, fades from view over time.

But over a period of some weeks, less than 25% of those supporters take part in this initial exercise much to everyone's disappointment. Why would people register their interest to join a new political party in Wales, but then turn up their noses at the opportunity to be part of the process to actually select the name of that party?

It's a bit baffling. Is this on-line malarkey all it's made out to be? The first deadline is extended to the end of February. Members are invited to list their three favourite names, with the proviso that the Steering Committee will still have the final say on the chosen name.

Altogether in the process, no fewer than seventy-two names are suggested. The list includes, Cymru Fydd, Cymru Newydd, Cymru Sofren, Democratic Party of Wales, Gwalia Patria, Liberty, One Nation, People's Movement of Wales, Gwalia, Libera Cambria, Pererin 2018, Tir a Mor, Amdani, Cymru Newydd, Ati, Torri'n Rhydd, Y Wawr, Ymlaen.

Although it is a drawn-out process, I enjoy it. I enjoy reading about the different suggestions and people's rationale for their choice of names, and like the fact that this is being done in such a participative way. I feel it augurs well for the kind of citizen-centred, participative democracy I would like to see the new party champion.

I'm also learning a lot from the exercise as well, for example the suggestion of Derwos, which apparently is the old Celtic name for Truth, and where the modern Welsh name of Derw (Oak) is derived.

I suggest Gwlad as my number one choice - which comes from the conclusion of the Welsh National Anthem, "Gwlad! Gwlad, Pleidiol wyf I'm Gwlad (Homeland, Homeland, I'm loyal to my homeland").

I flag up the huge and free PR the party could get every single time Wales play soccer or rugby. Basically, 70,000+ people would be singing the name of the new national party in front of an audience of some millions! I wonder how the BBC would cope with that....

Marketers say that that all companies and producers would do anything to engender a sense of pride, passion and trust in their products. Is there anything that engenders more trust and pride in the average Welshman or Welshwoman than pledging their allegiance to their own nation during the singing of the national anthem?

It's encouraging to see some supportive comments from other posters, such as Pendddu:

This name is widely recognized by even English speakers, apart from those lost causes who would never consider independence for Wales anyway. The subliminal effects of hearing "Gwlad! Gwlad" ring out when the anthems are played, would be priceless.

The whole process seems to be going down to the wire with new suggestions being made up, right to the deadline of February 23. It's particularly interesting to see names evoking Wales's landscape featuring strongly in this late surge. Yn ein Dwylo (In our hands), Tir a Mor (Land and Sea), and Dal dy Dir (Hold on to your land). I'm quite taken with these names since I just have a strong sense that we will have to depend much more on our land post-Brexit, in terms of growing food and utilizing it in new ways that can benefit people, both emotionally and physically.

I have a yen myself to re-engage with the land and involve myself in growing and nurturing things. We have family who farm in Dyffryn Conwy outside Conwy, where I and my two sisters spent a good deal of our childhood holidays. But, to be honest, I would probably make a lousy farmer.

Despite the drawn-out nature of the whole exercise, It's quite an exciting feeling to think that we are all part of a process to choose a name which will be presented to the whole Welsh nation in a few months down the line.

'Ger' sums it all up for all of us in his post:

I have had the same feelings as Eos Pegwern and Big Gee about the running process and 'over-democratising it'. However, I do think the naming exercise has thrown up some far more interesting names as a result, which is a big plus, IMO since the naming element is of such crucial importance.

I think the benefits of this long and frustrating process will be seen in the end, and we will all look back in future with a wry smile on our faces, having got to the finishing line with a result which we will say is a 'good un', even if it's not one of our personal favourites. It's easy to be critical of ourselves and the process, but I'd guess nobody ever asked their supporters what they should call the Labour Party, Plaid Cymru or probably any other party in the UK"

I miss the February meeting again due to work commitments, but I find out later that day that the name is going to be EIN GWLAD (Our Country). Passed by 4-2 at a below strength Steering Committee. There follow some recriminations.

I'm not particularly taken by the name immediately myself. I'm obviously chuffed that my original suggestion has been kept to some extent, but I'm not sure about the Ein placed in front of it. Big D doesn't like it either when I tell him.

He's been a bit sniffy about the whole venture from the start to be honest. He's got a sensitive antenna for these things, and he feels that it comes over as being too exclusionary.

But the name is duly released to the media and Welsh language website, Golwg 360 runs a story about the new party. Big Gee interviewed in his role as Chairperson is his usual combative and no-nonsense self. He starts by saying that Wales now needs a complete re-set following Brexit. Nothing wrong with that.

He then goes on to describe Plaid Cymru as being a "schizophrenic party," completely at odds with itself. I flinch when I read that because, living in such a politically-correct age, someone, somewhere was bound to complain.

A Golwg columnist by the name of Chris Dafis responds almost immediately to the article by saying that this choice of word was "offensive" and an insult to all people suffering from schizophrenia. He demands that Gwilym apologies for using the word. I actually laugh out loud when I read that comment. He obviously doesn't know Big Gee.

It's an absolutely ridiculous comment, typical of the 'right-on brigade' which are so prominent in modern Wales. As if every diagnosed schizophrenic in Wales would be mortally offended by being associated with PC in such a way. Was being compared to PC really that bad in Wales in 2018??! We all know that they have fallen into a perilous condition, but are they now an actual condition? And is referring to that condition off-limits?!!

In all seriousness though, for me it's a sign of how language is being manipulated and distorted today in the name of political correctness. I never fail to marvel how prophetic George Orwell was in his novel 1984 (written in 1954) with his description of how a language police would emerge to browbeat people into submission, passivity and obedience by controlling the use and mis-use of language.

The term 'schizophrenic' is surely a perfectly valid and generally understood term to use to describe an organisation beset by a whole host of internal contradictions. As Plaid Cymru undoubtedly are.

But, there are some other comments in the article which make me slightly more uncomfortable. Gwilym says that Ein Gwlad will stand up for the interests of Welsh people, but that will not include the influx of people from over the border (currently around 20% of the Welsh population). The wording in the article is a little awkward, and Gwilym says later that his words were taken out of context by the Golwg 360 reporter who spoke to him over the telephone. Golwg 360 have got form on this. Even so, it's a lesson to be learnt.

Of course it is indisputable that an influx of people from England has weakened the Welsh-speaking areas over the past two generations and is also now impacting on the more

English-speaking area of Wales as well. The nation's Welsh identity is undoubtedly under immense pressure in 2018. But even so, all nations have to accept outsiders. Outsiders are often those who bring in new ideas, new optimism and new dynamism to help the society and economy of their new country.

I encounter a graphic example of that myself some time later. I meet Svet, a Ukrainian lady who has just bought an old, run-down pub in Bangor, and has transformed it into a light, airy and friendly coffee shop and restaurant.

Svet already speaks five languages, Ukrainian, Russian, Polish, German and English, and is now hoping to learn Welsh as well. I teach her "Panad" (cup of tea) and "Bendigedig" (wonderful), to describe a very tasty Tomato and Pasta soup she has prepared herself.

She's only been here a few months, but she and her husband love it here. She says Gwynedd is so beautiful - more beautiful than even their last home at Hebden Bridge in Yorkshire - and the people are so friendly and open. Wales needs dynamic individuals such as Svet.

February 16th 2018

The grumblings about the Ein Gwlad name fester on. A couple of people on the web-forums say we should re-visit the matter at the March meeting of the SC, when more members will be present. This is met by a ferocious riposte from Big G. He accuses those members of being lilly-livered, and cowering before the opinions of the media at the very first hurdle. He's got a point in a way.

After all, it had been agreed that we were going to be different and refuse to play the usual game of trying to please the media, since there was a feeling that the media in Wales, similar to everywhere else had just become much too big for its boots. It had become some form of a monster with the range of its influence in modern society. It needs to be cut down to size and not dominate the political agenda to such an extent.

We had reached a consensus that being less subservient to the dictates of the media and to project ourselves in a much more direct and fearless manner would surely appeal to the Welsh public.

Big Gee threatens to walk away from the whole process if the name is changed. Despite my ringing ears after reading his no-holds barred e-mail, I must say that I sympathize with him. It would be an absolute disaster to change the name now after just having released it into the public domain. The party would just be a complete laughing stock.

He makes the entirely plausible point that any comparison with 'Ein Volk' of the Nazis in Germany should be laughed out of court immediately, as the meanings in German and Welsh are totally different. The German 'EIN' means 'ONE or THE', whilst the Welsh 'EIN' means 'OUR'.

I discover that EIN was actually introduced into the Welsh language by scholar William Salesbury in the second half of the 16th. Century. 2017 was the 450th anniversary of the translating the Bible into Welsh by Salesbury in 1567 - the act that actually saved the Welsh language as a living language and spared it from the fate of the other Celtic languages such as Gaelic, Irish and Cornish which had degenerated into a collection of local dialects without having such formal and official status for their own language. Salesbury introduced Ei, Ein and Eich into Welsh from the Latin equivalent 'Deius'.

It was an interesting notion to consider that William Salesbury lived during the first Brexit era in a way - when Henry VIII decided to break with Rome and set up an Independent Church of England entity.

With Britain having to fall back on its own resources and facing the ever-present threat of invasion from Catholic France and Spain, William Salesbury saw an opportunity to reference

Britain's ancient past and the role of the Welsh language in shaping that past in a new era of constructing a fresh identity for Britain, post-Rome.

He managed to persuade Henry V111 that publishing books in Welsh would be a way of emphasizing Britain's long and illustrious cultural and historical heritage in going its own way in the world. He was then granted a royal licence to publish four other Welsh language books in the 1550's - truly innovative works that were considered the equivalent of any other contemporary Humanist works in other European languages. Who knows, maybe the present Brexit - as confusing and disorderly as it is - can somehow herald a similar renaissance for the Welsh language .

I make a mental note to myself that should I ever find myself presented with a media knee-jerk reference to the 'EIN Volk' meme, I will ask them a counter-question. "So are you suggesting that the Welsh people have been racists for 1,500 years then?"

"How do you mean exactly?" the perplexed Journalist would counter I imagine.

"Well, "Ein Tad, yr hwn wyt yn y nefoedd"- (Our Father which art in Heaven) - has been in constant use here in Wales for that amount of time. "So, who is the racist? God himself or the Welsh people as a whole who have worshipped him for almost the entire existence of the Welsh nation itself"?

PEN PORTRAIT 4:

James Llewelyn-Henton:
Born Castell-Nedd. Now living in Aberystwyth.

I am a twenty-year-old student from Castell-Nedd (Neath). I come from a family with both industrial and agricultural backgrounds, and I'm now a student of International Politics and Intelligence Studies at the International Politics Department at Aberystwyth, which is the oldest of its kind in the world. I have always had a great interest in history which in turn led to my interest in politics during my teenage years.

I joined the effort to build what is now Ein Gwlad at it's very first meeting in late **2017**, during my first few months at Aberystwyth Uni aged nineteen. At that first meeting in the town's Morlan Centre, I volunteered for the Steering Committee and have been a part of it all ever since. What attracted me to go to the meeting and join was not only my old party's failings, but the fact I had been in talks just before I went to uni with people in Neath to set up a new Welsh party that could change the failed establishment, but that group never materialised into anything more. This all meant that when I saw an article advertising the first meeting in Aberystwyth for a party that is for all the people of Cymru that wanted change, I could not pass up the chance of being part of the better alternative for our great nation. Following that meeting I was not disappointed, and I soon left Plaid Cymru, as I knew that I had discovered the true party of Wales that day, in the foundation of what would become Ein Gwlad. The decision I made that day to be a part of this new alternative for Cymru is one I am greatly proud of, as I believe we can build Cymru into the nation it was always meant to be, someday.

In my view our Syncretic ideology is no doubt the way forward in the 21st century politics of Wales, as for far too long our nation has been divided and damaged by singular view ideologies that make up our current establishment. Politics and making a better nation are about more than being Left, Right or Centre after all. A modern system that can encompass all views from all sides of our nation's people is one that will make Cymru great. This new party is the only one that offers all people a place and hopefully we'll be able to soon achieve what all others have failed to do.

March 4th 2018

The Brexit debacle shows no sign of resolving itself soon. Personally, I wanted the Leave campaign to win because I have serious concerns about the lack of democracy and accountability within the European Union. It seems quite clear that the intended direction of travel is to obliterate national identities in Europe in favour of one super state in Brussels.

As a Welsh nationalist, I also wanted Brexit to happen because I felt that it would prove to be a revolutionary act as far as the governance of the UK was concerned. I saw it essentially as England's bid for Independence from the European Union. I believe such a development will inevitably lead to independence for Scotland and Wales in turn and a complete reconfiguration of the relationship between the three countries on this island.

This was very much a minority view within the nationalist community in Wales, which has an irrational adherence to the EU, seeing it as the fount of all progressivism and tolerance, and human rights etc. This attachment was akin to religious mania in some circles. Being against the EU was almost the mark of the devil in some places. These people literally could not see the distinction between the cultural and historical shared inheritance on the continent of Europe and the political construct of the European Union itself. It did certainly lead to the fraying of a couple of friendships along the way which proved to be troubling.

But, almost eighteen month down the line, the lack of clarity from the UK government as to the exact nature of Brexit was infuriating both Leavers and Remainers alike. Prime Minister's inane "Brexit means Brexit" was now beyond a joke. Theresa May was a Remainer who somehow found herself in charge of the process of negotiating the process of leaving the EU. It seemed clear that her strategy was to drag things out as long as possible, bore people to tears with the process so that we eventually end up in a situation of BRINO (Brexit in name only).

Her excruciatingly poor leadership skills and wooden speaking abilities just seemed to make everything ten times worse. It just beggared belief that arguably the biggest political development in UK politics since the last world war was being handled by such an incompetent. Theresa May seemed a metaphor for the complete diminution of Britain.

The Conservative Party was completely divided on the issue. The Labour Party likewise. Both parties along with the Lib Dems appeared to have been poleaxed by Brexit. It appeared to me that the whole political landscape we had inhabited for two generations and more had been transformed by Brexit.

It was also becoming increasingly obvious that the British Establishment (House of Commons, House of Lords, BBC, Civil Service, Whitehall, CBI etc) were doing their level best to undermine the referendum result and keep the UK as closely tethered to the EU as before the decision itself.

One study showed that 63% of constituencies throughout the UK had voted for Brexit. Parliament though was made up of 70% Remainers across the established parties. It was fast becoming a growing divide between the Politicians and People. Forget about Theresa May's crisis of leadership - this was fast becoming a crisis of democracy.

The ruling Metropolitan Liberal elite were doing their very best to vilify 'Leave' supporters as racist and ill-educated neanderthals who just couldn't see what was good for them. They managed to dress-up their own self-interest as some form of moral superiority.

This just seemed to increase people's anger with the whole establishment. After all, hadn't people voted to reject not only the EU but also the Westminster model of government which had served people so poorly everywhere outside the favoured areas of London and south east of England for a generation and more? With the politicians in Westminster mishandling of the process, I sensed a growing tide of resentment out there in society. This was not going to end well.

Interestingly, there was now talk of new parties being set up in England as well. A Democrats and Veterans party was the first out of the traps, closely followed by Engage. Over the next few months these were to be joined by Time. There was also fevered speculation that a new centrist, Europhile party could emerge in the new year, with figures such as former PM Tony Blair, Nick Clegg and Vince Cable of the Lib Dems involved. I was to hear more about this party from someone quite close to the proceedings in due course.

I wondered whether Ein Gwlad could make common ground with this groundswell of disillusion and anger amongst the people in England because of all Westminster's failings. Could that need for change prove to be a common determinant both in Wales and the rest of the UK? Could a new nationalist party in Wales link up our cause for national self-determination with the desire of other regions in England to have a fairer crack of the whip, post-Brexit?

And could that even be a way to slay the usual bugbear that had always plagued the Welsh national movement - that it was primarily motivated by anti-English sentiments. It was an interesting concept to ponder.

March 9th 2018

I manage to make it to the fourth meeting of EG at the same venue in Y Morlan, Aberystwyth. Gwilym, Royston, Gwyn, James are in attendance along with a newcomer, Gerald Gray, who apparently is now going to be the new secretary.

I find out that Gwyn comes from Cemaes Road, near Machynlleth. Typically, he knows a couple who are some of my parents' longest friends, Tom and Delyth Rees. That creates an instant link between us.Gwyn is as sharp as a tack. He runs a number of businesses, one of which involves selling clothes from a base in Macedonia to Belgium and the Netherlands, following his training in the textiles industry earlier in his career. He is a very good speaker, with a certain bullishness about him which makes him sound even more convincing every time he speaks.

He tells me that on occasions he had to do business with the disgraced business tycoon Philip Green. There had been a huge public outcry a few months previously concerning a pension scheme in one of his businesses which had proved worthless to his staff. Gwyn says that Phillip Green was an absolute b...... to deal with, accompanied as he was most times by two huge minders which made every meeting with him fraught with tension and menace.

Maybe some of Phillip Green's tactics has rubbed off on Gwyn since he certainly takes no prisoners. He knows exactly what he wants, and he's not shy about going for that. Gwyn usually regales us with one or two of his business stories at every meeting.

He tells us that he has a novel method to deal with customers who are loath to pay him or who are slow to respond to messages. He leaves an answerphone message along the lines of, "About this unpaid bill of £9,500 you owe me; can we discuss it please." The sum is obviously much less than this, but it works unfailingly, he says. His calls are always returned within an hour or so.

I pull his leg that he is the Phillip Green of Ein Gwlad. But there's another side to Gwyn as well as I am to find out in due course.

To my astonishment, Gwyn proposes that I become the Communications Officer for Ein Gwlad. I instantly regret bonding with him over the Cemaes Road connection. He wants me, the introverts' introvert to become the communications officer?! What is he thinking?

I know I have come to a place in my life when I seek to say 'Yes' to all new opportunities, but this is something else entirely. The rest of the group look expectantly at me. I've got to say something.

I try some of Gwyn's bullishness for size. I say categorically that I do not want to do any television or radio appearances in any such role. I'm hoping that will disqualify me immediately, but the rest seem completely unfazed by all that.

Assurances are made that other people will step up to the plate in that particular direction. I'm to concentrate on the writing element in Welsh and English and the general communications direction of Ein Gwlad. So, from being a complete bystander in the first meeting, I've somehow manged to find myself as the Communications Officer three months down the line.

Gwyn tells me that I can become the shadowy manipulator in the background. I quite like that idea to be honest. A kind of

Dr. No, influencing things in the shadows. Except, I've promised myself to be Dr Yes in life now. No, Yes, Yes, No - it's a kind of metaphor for my thinking about the actual prospects of Ein Gwlad at this point in time.

Sometimes I think we are completely deluded to think that this can actually come off, and that we all could be doing something much more productive with our lives. At other times, I'm actually persuaded that this is shaping up to be something transformational. There are other times when I'm stuck in the middle between the two positions, waiting to be swayed one way or the other.

We go through the agenda. Gwyn raises a problem with one of Gwilym's web-pages, explaining that it is quite difficult to use. It's not an unreasonable point but Gwilym rejects this complaint out of hand, without even giving it the time of day. Gwyn counters and the argument begins. The two Alpha Males of Ein Gwlad go head to head.

This toing and froing goes on for about ten minutes, with neither of the two giving ground. The rest of us sit there twiddling our thumbs, wishing we could be Alpha Males as well. Or probably not.

Gwyn and Gwilym's existential disagreement over some irrelevant point about whether a web page is easily accessible or not rumbles on. They are like two stags on some windswept heath, horns locked together in mortal combat. Not one of them gaining an inch at all; but no one losing an inch neither. It goes on and on. And on.

Finally Gwilym relents and says that he will have a look at the offending site. Gwyn has triumphed. I'm just glad that he doesn't avail himself of the proprietal rights usually afforded to the dominant male stag amongst the watching herd after such a victory.

March 16ᵗʰ 2018

Social Media. We've all agreed that this has to be an essential part of our communications strategy, and we are very lucky to have Darren Owen from Caerffili on the case for us. I usually do my best to avoid social media, but I acknowledge that this has to be done. Over the next few months, Darren starts up an Ein Gwlad Facebook account and a Twitter account in order to communicate our message to the Welsh public.

With no party actually yet in existence, it's a hard sell in one sense, but Das goes about the work with gusto, later joined by Lee Felton of Cydweli, another proficient social media operative. Their combined efforts were to become an invaluable resource over the next few months.

I'm not a big fan of social media, if truth be told. I'm not on Facebook or Twitter, despite my daughter's concerted attempts to convert me. It just seems to promote and thrive upon this new culture of continual outrage and tends to bring the worst out in people for some reason. As someone said: " People you might have disagreed with ten years ago - now they just seem unhinged".

I experience this for myself. We are in the middle of a huge media story, the "Me Too" campaign, which has exploded on the media following revelations about the sexual misconduct of a powerful Hollywood mogul, Harvey Weinstein. One or two complaints about his behaviour over the years lead to a floodgate of complaints, all of which are covered extensively by the media.

There are no doubt serious allegations of rape in their midst. But 'Me Too' immediately strikes me as being very narcissistic in itself - emanating as it does from the very centre of narcissity itself, Hollywood. There's more than a touch of 'Too Me' to the campaign, and a shrillness, stridency and a black and white thinking to it that I find very disturbing. There's a sense that all men are being tarred with the same brush with little or no nuance allowed. Modern feminism seems to have taken a dark turn.

I write a Welsh language blog about the issue for Golwg 360 with the title: '*A yw ffeministiaeth wedi troi'n ffeministiaith*'- it's a play on words asking whether modern feminism has now developed into its own exclusive language to deal with modern life.

I acknowledge all the positive changes which have taken place within society over the past generation or so affording better opportunities for all women. But, I suggest that the "Me Too" campaign, fuelled by highly-paid Hollywood actresses and their lawyers eyeing up a small fortune in future court compensation should be treated with some scepticism.

I also suggest that waging war on men in this way is not a good idea for society. It's almost as if all nuances in the complex and life-affirming relationship dance between men and women are to be cast aside. Are we indeed entering a phase where there is a wish to even criminalize all male sexual initiative?

'*Surely, George Orwell's Anti-Sex League in their boiler suits can't be far behind?*' I write.

Within a day or so, the sisterhood strike back. An academic, called Dani Edwards-Behr from Aberystwyth University launches a blistering rebuttal - more or less confirming my suggestions that some elements of modern feminism had indeed become slightly 'unhinged'. Golwg 360, for some bizarre reason runs her article under the heading, 'Erthygl greulon ac anghyfrifol Aled Gwyn Job.' (Aled Gwyn Job's cruel and irresponsible article). The academic claims that 'Me Too' is a totally liberating and empowering movement, and a long-needed attack on male privilege and hierachy which has held women back for so long. She sounded completely convinced of the rightness of her argument, I must say.

But, this idea of collective guilt and complicity on one side of the equation and collective hurt and injustice on the other side was troubling. Could individual cases involving men and women really be treated on their own merits under such circumstances? And was this new sexual politics also being used for blatant partisan purposes?

All this came into sharp focus some months down the line at a hearing to consider whether a Republican nominee for the Supreme Court in America was guilty of historic sexual misbehaviour against a Professor named Christine Ford, aligned with the Democratic Party. The whole of America seemed fixated with a case which essentially boiled down to whether one teenager had groped another teenager at a drunken party thirty-six years ago. Thirty-six years ago! An incident which was not even related to her close friends or parents in its wake, and no complaint ever filed with the Police. But now this incident had been dredged up from the past to be used as a sexual harassment charge against the nominee for the Supreme Court, Brett Kavanaugh.

"Believe the women," was the cry of the protestors who congregated outside the hearings. I'd always thought that justice was all about "Believe the evidence". But, maybe I'm just old-fashioned like that.

It was more than a little ironic therefore that over the summer, a 'Me Too' leader in America, the actress Asia Angezo, who had made many accusations against Harvey Weinstein, found herself the subject of such allegations herself.

It was revealed that she paid a sum of $390,000 to buy the silence of a 17-year-old young actor, Jimmy Bennett who accused her of sexually exploiting him in a hotel room in California in 2014.

The age of consent in California is 18. Jimmy Bennet decided to go public about his experiences after suffering emotional trauma in the following years after the incident. Now maybe most normal 17-year-old teenagers would love to be seduced by an older woman. But who knows in this case.

Maybe this whole 'Me Too' issue is not so black and white after all......

My own trial by media doesn't end with Golwg 360. S4C's 'Hansh' programme runs a video message by a Lisa Angharad, looking very cool in a red beret, who launches into another attack calling me a sad middle-aged misogynist who has lost the plot entirely. I don't watch it myself, but friends tell me it's pretty strong stuff.

I find it mildly amusing to be the subject of such outrage. Tesni on the other hand is outraged by the slurs and thinks she needs to protect her father's honour. She composes a passionate Facebook post responding to Lisa Angharad saying that I have always encouraged her to believe herself to be equal to men in every respect and able to achieve anything she wants in life. She even says that I introduced her to the Suffragette movement etc! I'm really touched by her post, She's even corralled a huge amount of her friends to back me up on the Facebook page!

But it doesn't end there. I have a long and passionate exchange about my article with my landlord where I work in Caernarfon, Selwyn Jones. I have a huge respect for Sel as he is known, for his years of work with 'Cymdeithas yr Iaith' (Welsh language society). He's also been the driving force behind 'Llety Arall' (An Alternative Accommodation) which is going to be a centre for Welsh learners in Caernarfon.

The idea with 'Llety Arall' is that learners from all parts of Wales can come to stay at the bunkhouse for periods of time and practice their Welsh in the most Welsh-speaking place in the whole of Wales, Caernarfon (86% Welsh-speaking). It's a great idea. Wales had its own language learning centre at Nant Gwrtheyrn near Pwllheli. But Nant Gwrtheyrn, for all its excellent work, was a centre set apart from the world, based as it was in a disused old quarry village. Llety Arall on the other hand will be based right in the centre of a living Welsh community, where Welsh language reigns supreme.

Sel spearheaded the campaign to crowdfund this vision and managed to persuade local people to fork out £150,000 towards the project. Vision and determination. A great combination to have.

But Sel is someone who you could also perhaps describe as being a keen supporter of the Authoritarian Left.

Sel tells me in Y Blac Boi pub that my article is totally, totally out of order. "Me Too" is a liberating force for women he argues- and any arguments to the contrary are just reactionary. And probably Tory as well. And just plain wrong all round.

I tell him that I have also written a supplementary article in English on the subject on nation.cymru to develop the discussion somewhat. He tells me he doesn't want to read it. It's not going to change his mind. He's right and I'm wrong.

I quote George Orwell at him: *"True liberty has to mean the right to tell people things they don't want to hear"*, but it cuts no ice.

I've always felt that Sel and I, for all our differences, were really not too far apart on the important issues in life, with him looking at life through the prism of the left and I looking at life through the prism of faith. But, this is different. I'm shocked and shaken with his attitude to be honest. It changes things between us.

Get used to being a Communications Officer. Its sure to be a foretaste of the kind of attitudes that will be displayed towards Ein Gwlad before long.

It's no wonder people keep their heads down in Wales, I think. If you do ever put your head above the parapet at all to express an alternative view- get ready for a fusillade of shots to be aimed towards you.

Maybe I am naïve to hope that Ein Gwlad can be a vehicle to challenge this state of affairs. I want to see a thriving democracy where people can express their opinions openly and honestly, whatever those opinions are. Let all schools of thought contend and let the best triumph through open debate and consideration!

PEN PORTRAIT 5

Mike Murphy:
Born in Cardiff: Presently living in Siberia.

My name is Mike Murphy, born in Cardiff in <u>1961</u> and raised in Bridgend. At that time the local council, as with many across southern Wales, was fiercely anti-Welsh. I initially believed that the Welsh name for Bridgend was Langenau – Bridgend's twin town in Germany · whose name was given prominence on sign posts to the exclusion of Penybont. Because to add Penybont would be expensive and distract drivers....

It was this stupid contradiction which first made me interested in the Welsh language and Welsh nationalism generally, and I gradually became a fervent believer in the cause of Welsh independence. I became an active web·warrior under the name of Penddu but was very disillusioned with the established political parties and did not become actively engaged in party politics until Ein Gwlad.

In real·life I am a civil engineer who has spent many years travelling the world building oil and gas plants. My current assignment has me working alternate months in Russia, where many of Ein Gwlad's tweets have originated, and I hope this has raised a few eyebrows in MI6....

April 12th 2018

With the name conundrum seemingly resolved once and for all, we can finalise the arrangements concerning the logo. Once again, this discussion has proved to be a lively and frank exchange of views between supporters on the forum, lasting over two months in all, as different ideas are thrown into the pot.

We already have of course, the registered emblems which have been promised to us by Ioan Richard, the councillor who nearly drove us all to despair at that initial meeting in November. Those emblems are the Welsh Dragon and a map of Wales - although there are questions about the accuracy of the map in question since a section of north-east Wales has somehow disappeared from it.

The dragon of course is emblematically Welsh and immediately recognisable throughout Wales and beyond. Big Gee has already started up a new logo thread on the forum and some quite imaginative designs have been submitted. There's one of a magnificent golden dragon and there's another of a dragon bursting out of its limiting chains.

The problem with the Welsh Dragon of course is that it has become appropriated by all and sundry in Welsh national life to the extent of becoming by now almost a meaningless corporate brand. Anyone who wants to claim any form of Welshness, however spurious, will slap a Welsh dragon on their company branding. From Visit Wales to Cardiff City FC to the Scarlets to the Welsh Government itself, it had quite simply been flogged to death.

Its motto: 'Y ddraig Goch ddyry gychwyn' (the Welsh Dragon starts on its way) had now degenerated into 'Y ddraig goch ddyry ddychryn' (the Welsh Dragon would be appalled) to see the way its potency, fire and rebelliousness had now been shoehorned into a tame, corporate blandness in modern Welsh life.

Quite simply, the brand itself had been tarnished and tainted. There was general agreement amongst the group and more widely on the forum in time, that another approach was needed.

An alternative suggestion then came to light, the use of Ivy for our logo. There is of course huge symbolic significance to the Ivy. Ivy had been placed on the severed head of Llywelyn Ein Llyw Olaf (Llywelyn the Last), the last leader of an independent Wales, and paraded around London as a symbol of Edward 1's systematic smashing of Welsh Independence in 1282. The Ivy draped around the Ein Gwlad name was certainly a potent and powerful statement.

Some, including myself could see the potency and the beauty of the Ivy but there was a fear that this was too backward-looking. I could anticipate the naysayers announcing that Ein Gwlad were referencing an event that took place 800 years ago, which had no real relevance for modern Wales. It could also lead to claims that the new party were fostering an out-and-out anti-English agenda.

Stephen Morris, in his usual incisive manner, nailed it in a post on February 27:

"We don't want to look as if we are settling an 800-year grudge. We first have to achieve independence without alienating those whose support we need; there is plenty of time to teach people about their history after that."

The brickbats were bound to come our way whatever. These brickbats were being prepared at that very moment. Why add to the number of brickbats?

A third option then emerges. This option seems to have immediate traction.

It's the Phoenix: the bird which self-combusts every few hundred years and then re-emerges from its own ashes to fly free again.

Ger, who came up with the idea on a very apt date- St. David's Day on March 1 - puts it like this:

We all know the tale of the bird that regenerates itself to its former glory from its own ashes. The essence is reincarnation, renewal, re-

birth - analogous I feel to what we agreed with Ein Gwlad - trying to build Cymru from the metaphorical wasteland it has become ."

The obvious symbolism - Wales rising from the ashes - appeals to every one of us.

Two designers are set to work on the work and we agree to come to a conclusion by next month's steering committee meeting.

This collaborative on-line effort proves to be much more focused and direct than the name-choosing exercise undertaken a couple of months earlier. Key lessons had been learnt. One of those lessons was that the name-choosing process had been much too loose and diffuse.

It was great that everybody was pitching in with their ideas, but the scatter-gun nature of that process meant that the exercise went on for much too long. Collaborative thinking could be more precise surely?

It perhaps showed that one person should lead on the issue. We were lucky that Mike Murphy (Penddu) took the lead on this. Mike is a civil engineer working out in Siberia of all places. But even though he was based on the other side of the world, he was able to provide the direction and drive that was needed on this process.

A few weeks later Mike (Penddu) presented the final logos for inspection, and both were passed unanimously by the Steering Committee. The Phoenix it is.

Arth Ddu speaks for all of us:

"A nation arising from its sleep. The way that the head is pointed upwards and the stretched wide wings, are clear messages that we, the people are arising to meet the challenges facing Wales."

Big Gee even goes as far as to say that he feels the logo beats all existing logos used by every political party on these isles.

The coloured version will be the logo be used for Ein Gwlad's general literature, leaflets, cards, posters etc. The black and white version will be the emblem used for the purposes of the ballot papers, as required by the Electoral Commission.

When those ballot papers are prepared for the 2021 Election, the name Ein Gwlad will be the first party to appear on the ballot paper. A huge advantage one would guess.

April 16th 2018

Ein Gwlad suffer a good many hiccups along the way as regards its personnel. First to go is Alan Hughes, the Welsh-speaking Glaswegian near Dolgellau who had been given the role of national secretary on the Steering Committee. In his resignation letter to Big Gee says that family commitments mean that he can't devote the time to fully carry out his role as national secretary.

But, he also says that he found the tone of the Golwg 360 article, problematical for an 'outsider' such as himself. Big Gee tries to dissuade him, pointing to the fact that he has gone to the effort of learning Welsh and integrating into the community near Dolgellau. But Alan has made his mind up, and all Gwilym's pleadings fall on deaf ears.

The next to go is Gerald Gray, after only a month in situ as the secretarial successor to Alan Hughes. Gwilym is implicated again. But it's an odd affair all round.

The renegade politician Neil McEvoy had been in constant contact with Gwilym and Royston by phone over some weeks discussing the political situation in Wales and the emergence of Ein Gwlad, and it was eventually agreed for them to meet up at a pub in Neath to discuss matters.

Gerald is invited along as the new national secretary. Gerald is apparently under the impression that this is to be a secret meeting with no publicity afforded to it at all. That in itself struck me as being a highly unlikely state of affairs, considering the fact that the meeting involved perhaps the most publicity-seeking politician in Wales in Neil McEvoy. But perhaps that's being unfair to the ex-Plaid Cymru politician, Lord Elis Thomas.

Following the meeting, which by all accounts was a positive and constructive meeting, Gwilym posts up a short report for the members on the forum. It's a useful account of what transpired at the meeting.

But Gerald sees this and considers it to be a blatant breaking of what he sees as a personal assurance given to him and promptly resigns. We've lost two secretaries in close succession.

Gerald pens a formal and lengthy letter of resignation. It's almost as if he's a cabinet minister submitting his resignation letter to our Theresa May. He follows the usual protocol of thanking Gwilym and the SC for the opportunity to serve and wishes all of us well for the future. It's all a bit bizarre. Was Gerald on a fishing trip on behalf of someone or other? The Welsh Labour party maybe?

It doesn't ring true somehow. It's not as if the report of the meeting was being broadcast from the rooftops to all and sundry. It was merely a report to other registered members on the Ein Gwlad forum. Gerald seems to have thrown his toys out of the pram almost before the pram was ever in motion.

The secretarial pram was to remain unmanaged for several months. Gwilym as usual had to pick up the slack.

But, in an odd way, the two resignations so close together, rather than leading to a crisis of confidence within the Steering Committee, seems to bolster resolve. The remaining five members of the Steering Committee have to buckle down even more, and it seems to be working.

It's an odd thing to say - but we're almost becoming some sort of family by now. Sure, there's the usual bickering and grumbles that are par for the course in any family - but there's also a close bond building up between us. A sense that we are in this for the long run and we have to look out for each other.

We are almost like a band of brothers. But that in itself is becoming problematical.

Royston voices concerns that, although we have a good few females on the forum, not one female has come forward to become a member of the Steering Committee. He says it's a weakness that has to be resolved.

Big Gee begs to differ. He's so anti PC, he's almost off the scale. It's quite refreshing I must say.

His argues that whatever the dictates of modern society may be, you can't trump biology. Men, he says have traditionally been the leaders, taking the lead in war, diplomacy and politics, because of biological imperatives. Women on the other hand, by nature are more nurturing and caring and have a different set of skills entirely.

He dismisses this current fad to want 50/50 balance in the National Assembly as a completely ridiculous concept. He says we don't need to concern ourselves with this issue at all. Females will find their level within Ein Gwlad naturally without us having to be tokenistic at all, he says.

I think Gwilym is on to something here, but I don't accept his premise entirely. We quite obviously do need more females on the Steering Committee, we require different ways of looking at things and a female perspectives on how we are doing And anyway, I'm getting fed up at looking at Royston, Gwilym, James and Gwyn all the time! They are not oil paintings any one of them to be honest. Any more than I am at my age, either.

My experience with YES Cymru Caernarfon - part of the new non-party aligned movement started up a year previously, YES Cymru - also leads me to believe that things could be different. Since its inception last August, the meetings of that group have always attracted many women and group feels very balanced and modern as a result. YES Cymru are obviously doing something right.

I wonder whether it is the fact that YES Cymru are beyond conventional politics to all intents and purposes, as they do not wish to align themselves to any political party. Maybe the fact that they are pursuing a course which goes beyond the usual political scene is the very reason why they are attracting so many women into their ranks. YES Cymru are coming along in leaps and bounds with new groups appearing all over Wales.

Taking their inspiration from the YES Scotland movement, which made such an impression during the Scottish Independence referendum of 2014 and now gearing up again for a possible second referendum, YES Cymru are putting the case for Welsh Independence in a fresh and vibrant manner. They seemed to put all the political parties in Wales to shame with their energy and enthusiasm.

They were tapping into a creativity and vision which devolution had seemingly throttled since its inception in 1999. They were the ones who seemed to be tapping into the anti-political meme which had developed apace over the past few years.

YES Caernarfon had organized 'Annibynwyl' (Indy Fest) to mark Owain Glyndwr day in Caernarfon the previous September. That had been organized organically by a collection of the members. It had been an impressive example of co-production.

Throughout this period I maintain my connection to YES Cymru by means of the YES Caernarfon group, who had some excellent and committed individuals in its ranks. But I remain convinced that political power had to be achieved through the ballot box as well, thus the need for Ein Gwlad who were committed to seek that type of power.

I dream of a coalition between the two organisations. I even come up with a name for the new entity: YES GWLAD. Not grammatically correct, but potent perhaps.

As our objectives are so closely aligned ,we agree that we need to meet up with YES Cymru as soon as possible. We have to wait a couple of months for that first meeting and when it eventually happens it leads to a major fall-out which threatens to scupper any talk of co-operation between the two organisations.

April 19th 2018

I travel to Liverpool for the Association in the North's meeting at Bethel Church, one of the three Welsh-speaking Churches still in existence in the city - a remnant of that time when Welsh men and women poured into Liverpool to find work in the 19th and 20th century, and when the city was known as the capital of north Wales.

There, I meet the famous Rev D Ben Rees, who has been a minister in the city for over forty years, and still has care of three churches. D Ben Rees is a force of nature who has managed to rack up no fewer than nine degrees during his career. He has also written countless books, including several biographies of notable Welsh politicians such as the former Welsh Secretaries of State, Jim Griffiths and Cledwyn Hughes.

He's not so mobile as he used to be, but he's lost none of his razor-like wit and his willingness to express his views forthrightly. It's typical of him that he takes to the podium on the very first day to show this fearlessness once again.

He mentions the case of a former general secretary who used to phone him up almost nightly to try and persuade him to retire - so as to provide new opportunities within the denomination for younger people. He then goes on to mention the fact that this particular individual has now just retired from his ministerial post with the denomination.

"*But who do we now find has landed himself another job within the Church as an administrator*" he asks mischievously. "*The very same person!*"

The audience wince visibly, knowing that Dr Ben has hit the mark once again. But after delivering this excocet, he reverts to being his usual jovial self, and all the tension in the room dissipates immediately. It's a classic Dr Ben performance.

As we have a loose family connection (he was in attendance at my parents' wedding) I manage to wangle myself a lift in Dr Ben's impressive Jaguar car to a service in one of his three churches.

The conversation turns to politics. The Welsh Labour Leader Carwyn Jones has just announced that he is to stand down from his post as leader later this year. Although it is a well-known secret that he was to stand down before the next Assembly elections in 2021 - it's obvious that the Carl Sergeant tragedy has speeded up the process.

There are two inquiries launched into the events leading up to his suicide. It really doesn't look good for Carwyn Jones that a process instigated and overseen by him led to the suicide of a fellow Labour politician. He's obviously been tainted by the event and he's looking for some damage limitation.

Dr Ben with his links to the Labour Party is obviously up to speed with all the developments. He tells me that Mark Drakeford is the obvious frontrunner for the post. But he also suggests that Baroness Eluned Morgan, also from Cardiff, could be a dark horse to watch.

He also tells me that his son Dafydd Rees, who works in PR in London, is also working on a huge project at present. I don't have to coax it out of him. Dr Ben is in full flow. He tells me that Dafydd is advising Tony Blair, Alistair Campbell and Peter Mandelson concerning starting up a new pro-European party to oppose Brexit.

I'm quite enjoying my journey in the big Jaguar and I don't want to dent Dr Ben's enthusiasm for all this by telling him that I absolutely detest those three politicians. I could have piped up to say how, in my opinion, those three have been responsible for polluting political life in the UK over the past generation. But I don't.

And obviously, I keep schtum about my little venture into the political arena. But, I file that very interesting fact away about the new party for use at a later date.

At the very time of my visit to Liverpool, I hear that a relative of mine, who has been researching into the family tree has uncovered a missing part of the family jigsaw. She has found out what happened to a great-great-grandfather of ours, David Roberts, who had somehow disappeared from the family story. Nia has found out that he actually died in the West Derby Poorhouse at the age of 50 in 1881. Of liver failure. A heavy drinker, obviously.

Up to this point, my mother and the rest of the family never knew the full story about her grand-father. Having left a widow and ten-year-old daughter to fend for themselves in Liverpool, his story remained untold when his wife and daughter eventually returned to the family farm in Wales ten years later. Was it shame, embarrassment, or just a more understandable human desire to protect close family members from an inconvenient truth?

I get quite emotional about this discovery, staying as I am in a hotel not all that far away from where the West Derby Poorhouse used to stand. I think it just tells me, once again, and quite forcibly as well- you've got to get going in life.

It's also speaks of an unspoken history when it comes to the traditional Welsh narrative. I've been attending a church gathering and paying tribute to the Welsh church tradition in Liverpool. My great-great grandfather would no doubt have had an association with one of the myriad of Welsh churches in Liverpool at that time.

Did his church provide any support or succour to him during his illness I wonder? Did they offer any support to his bereaved wife and daughter? Not very likely I think. The churches in Liverpool, like the rest of Wales indeed were bastions of middle-class respectability and decorum. People like David Roberts and his ilk, who failed to keep to these standards of behaviour were more often than not, seen to be beyond the pale.

Welsh Non-conformism for all its achievements was essentially a top-down institution, and a flawed institution at that. Like all other Church institutions, it was a long, long way away from the nature of the bottom-up early church mentioned in the Book of Acts. Faith had become swallowed up by an institution.

"Life was really tough for the ordinary Welshman and Welshwoman in Liverpool at that time," says Big D when I tell him about the family discovery. "They were treated like serfs; their poverty and hardship has never been part of the Welsh narrative about life in Liverpool".

The story of David Roberts seems to be a symbol for the countless other untold stories in the Welsh experience over the years. His airbrushing out of the family history for so long seems a metaphor for how the Welsh themselves have been airbrushed out of history in these isles over the centuries.

The Liverpool connection finds another link when I mention my visit to Liverpool to Gwilym. He tells me that his second wife comes from Birkenhead, and he visits there quite regularly. He tells me that he feels an instinctive warmth towards Liverpudlians - and that perhaps they are closer to the Celts in the rest of these isles than the Anglo-Saxons who dominate political, economic and cultural life.

Liverpool, and other regions in England seem so different to the Liberal Metropolitan elite based in London and the South-east of England. I feel sorry for such places. At least Wales has a national identity as a base for our wish to be freed from their rule. The proud regions of England have no such recourse of course. But, I wonder again whether a resurgent national identity for Wales can be good for those regions as well?

April 25th 2018

Any new party has to have a Constitution in place which will then form a central plank of the eventual registration with the Electoral Commission. The Constitution will be the highest authority within the party, so this has to be done properly. It's not my cup of tea at all. It's a dry, painstaking and laborious process which takes organised and methodical minds to make it work properly. That's not me.

The task is delegated to Stephen Morris 'Eos Pengwern' and Mike Murphy 'Penddu'. I had encountered the two of them on-line way before we met up in real life. I very much admired the penmanship of the two of them on various on-line forums, both presenting their arguments with eloquence and passion. The two, along with Mike Powell from Y Rhondda, work collaboratively on the constitution by means of Skype and by April they have come up with constitution that is more or less complete.

The Aims and Values of Ein Gwlad are outlined as follows:
Independence: To establish a free, sovereign and independent Welsh state.
Accountability: To secure a government which is democratically accountable to the people of Wales.

Prosperity: To bring about a flourishing Welsh economy where all citizens have the opportunity to prosper and where enterprise and hard work are properly rewarded.

Distinctiveness: To secure a future for our national language, distinctive heritage, traditions and culture.

Internationalism: To see Wales takes its place among the community of nations fostering good relations and mutually beneficial links with other states around the world.

It will be another two months before I meet Dr. Stephen Morris. But his reputation precedes him. Stephen lives over the border in Shrewsbury and has a PhD in something to do with reflectionary materials. He worked in Silicon Valley before setting up his own company in Cardiff and is now working in the world of producing medical devices.

Stephen has proved a very valuable and committed contributor on the forum, quite apart from his methodical work on the constitution and he offers to write an article about Ein Gwlad for the nation.cymru website. He may be a scientist, but he writes like a dream.

'Introducing Ein Gwlad: A Unique Party seizing a Unique Opportunity' is the heading he chooses for the article.

'For 1,500 years we have been living cheek by jowl with one of the most expansionist cultures on the planet, yet while retaining our distinctiveness,' he writes.

He highlights Wales's historical uniqueness by pointing to the fact that Wales was the first country in Europe to codify its laws, the first to develop its industry and the first to educate its people.

But he argues that its political and national life is now at a complete impasse, having fallen behind in educational standards, living standards and other indicators of well-being over the twenty years of devolution. He says that both the ruling party Welsh Labour, and Plaid Cymru, who are so closely aligned to Welsh Labour have failed Wales over many, many years.

"We are a new party which is committed to make Wales the country that its people deserve it to be. First and foremost, that means an unequivocal commitment to independence."

Gwyn gets the bright idea to collate all the responses to the article and to identify some of the common themes that emerge. It's important to get a handle on all the possible objections and scepticism about the emergence of a new party. Firstly, to try and understand people's initial reactions to the development. But more importantly, to try and respond to those concerns in a constructive manner.

Amongst the objections we find:

Richard Jenkins
Shame to split vote
Future same as divisive past
Divide and rule
Work with the only credible party (PC) ....credible chance
Doing a UKIP
Public opinion is anti-Brexit now
Stick with Plaid and YES CYMRU
Ben Jones
Lib Dems can deliver Home Rule
Plaid further away now than in 70s...had 90 years
Tony Coslett
YES CYMRU ...destroying the lies
Paul Sambrook
Going nowhere, seen it all before
Morgan Owen Bowler-Brown
Taking votes away from Plaid
Support YES CYMRU
Sulk off and form another party
Arthur Davies
Based on negativity (hatred of Labour)

Failing to get your own way in PC

Aims no different to PC

"radical" Independence is radical, PC is for that

Pragmatic = bit by bit devolution

Unacceptable comments re. immigrants (Golwg 360)

Roger Harris

Majority is monoglot English speakers

David Jones

Why has NM not joined Ein Gwlad

Steve Duggan

Stop infighting

Chris Franks

"reduce role of Public Sector"=goodbye to NHS and State education

Leigh Richards

"opportunities by Brexit" ...what are they?

Andrew Morgan, James Humphreys, Nicholas Daniels all positive

Tony Coslett

Joined YES CYMRU + Propel Cymru, the way forward

It's a very useful exercise. All these comments will be taken into consideration for the next article which will be prepared. Big Gee suggests that we write another article for Nation.cymru rebutting the points that were raised. But we reach a consensus that we shouldn't be driven by other people's knee-jerk reaction and give the impression of being precious. It's agreed we should focus on making a positive case for Ein Gwlad when the next opportunity arises. As it happens, we don't have to wait too long.

We receive an invitation to write an article about Ein Gwlad for the Welsh language paper Y Cymro at the National Eisteddfod in Cardiff in August. When that occasion arises, we decide to compile the article on the basis of some of the objections raised following Stephen's article.

PEN PORTRAIT 6

Dr.Stephen Morris:
Born in Pwllheli. Now living near Shrewsbury

Since many years, I have been frustrated that the
only party which stood for Independence in Wales –
albeit in a very half-hearted fashion - Plaid
Cymru, also stands for a number of other things
that I could never believe in: socialism, political
correctness, membership of the EU, political
"bullying" and other such things which are totally
contrary to the native Welsh culture. As much as I
would like to see Welsh an Independent nation, it
could hardly be described as "free" under such a
government. Under such circumstances, an
Independent Wales would be poorer, less free and in
a worse condition than she is today.

It would seem that the above elements were just
as obvious to **80%** of the Welsh electorate. It was
also clear that Plaid Cymru had reached the high
point of their support and there was no hope of
winning Independence by an increase in the level of
electoral support for Plaid.

The only way therefore to increase the vote for
Independence is to have another party to reach out
to the **80%** (who are either economically liberal -
and therefore vote for the Tories) or socially
conservative (who went to UKIP in **2010** and
especially in **2015**), or who see no reason to leave
the Labour party which is still the default
position in many parts of Wales, despite its abject
failure to improve things here after a century in
power.

Therefore, it was totally clear to me that Wales needed a brand new political party: one which would stand firmly for Independence, not like PC, and which at the same time could propose policies which would make Wales a prosperous and free country and provide real hope to improve people's life opportunities here - not like the Labour party; avoiding being cowed by England and the British Establishment - not like the Tories and UKIP; without falling into "jingoistic nationalism" or worse like some of the smaller nationalist groups in England.

After following the 'Jac o the North' blog and discovering the nation.cymru website, I realised I was not on my own in thinking like this, and that there was a core of other people who had reached their own conclusions about the situation and who had a vision for Wales's future. From this point on, it was clear that it was my duty to do whatever I could to ensure the opportunity was not missed.

May 1st 2018

I find myself taking a few services locally as part of my New Leaders course with the Presbyterian Church of Wales. It is increasingly the case that the congregations are very small - less than 15 is the norm - and increasingly elderly. It's now becoming a matter of some wonderment to see anyone beneath fifty in attendance. Even children, who at one stage used to attend Sunday School up to the age of eleven before drifting away in their teenage years, as my own daughter had done, are now absent on the whole. There's an air of hopelessness surrounding the remaining faithful few in the pews. The whole structure is crashing down all around us. Of that, there is no doubt at all.

As a denomination, the Presbyterian Church Of Wales is losing 5% membership every year. We are now less than 20,000 in number. A television documentary a few months previously had shown that there had been a 68% decline in numbers since

1990 - we had lost more members than any other denomination in Wales since 1990 . Even those pesky Independents were ahead of us in the numbers game by now!

There had always been a keen sense of competition between the Presbyterians and the Independents in Wales. Even if Church of Wales membership was still way ahead (on 45,000), there always seemed to be a sense that "God's in his heaven and all's right with the world" as long as we were ahead of the Independents. Now that little moral advantage had been overturned. It's ridiculous I know, but it did seem to put salt on the numbers wound.

Meirion Morris, my University contemporary and General Secretary tried to put on a brave face in the television interview- but the worry and concern about this unprecedented decline in numbers was deeply etched on his face. Everything seemed hopeless.

This was a period where there seemed to be news of church scandals concerning historic child abuse breaking every other week. To many, it seemed that the Catholic Church had been a haven for paedophiles for many, many years, with church leaders failing completely in their duty to protect innocent children. There was a revulsion against the Church in many countries, especially Ireland whose Abortion referendum later in the year seemed more than anything else to be a huge popular vote against the Catholic Church and its historic influence in Ireland.

We were lucky in Wales that there were no equivalent child abuse scandals in our churches. Although there was that bizarre case of one Presbyterian minister who for some reason got his kicks by dissecting a particular part of the male anatomy from bodies he encountered as part of his work. It was a huge scandal at the time and very distressing for the families concerned. But in general, there wasn't the same sense of revulsion towards the church here in Wales as was the case in

Ireland. Not that made any difference to church figures of course.

And yet. And yet. I still feel there is something beyond this tale of absolute decline and decay. Perhaps indeed the whole edifice had to come to an end for something completely new and different to take its place… like a phoenix raising up from the ashes.

My mentor, the irrepressible Rev Harri Parri, although in his 80s is as modern as they come in his thinking about most things and he was now talking about welcoming a 'new slate' scenario. With perhaps one or two new generations in Wales with no contact with traditional churches at all, the old prejudices, personal grievances and hang-ups about faith were not really there anymore. A new generation, completely untouched by the past, could see things differently perhaps, he ventures.

I see traces of that myself by taking part in the 'Open The Book' project in three schools in Caernarfon. 'Open The Book' is a project which sees church members going into schools to act out a few Biblical stories. The response of the pupils is wonderful. The majority of them have never heard of these stories, but they really respond well to them. The headteachers tell us that their pupils really enjoy the stories and look forward tremendously to our fortnightly visits.

This all coincides with the rise and rise in the media of a Canadian academic named Jordan Peterson. Peterson was termed controversial because of his willingness to challenge some of the agenda of the liberal technocracy in the West. A psychologist by training, he had recently recorded a number of videos named 'The Psychological Significance of the Stories of the Bible'. His talks attract huge audiences with a large number also watching them later on the internet. Peterson is undoubtedly a fantastic public speaker.

What's particularly striking that the majority of the attendees at his talks are young people - mostly young men. These people aren't in our churches any more - but Peterson's influence seemed to indicate that there was a huge hunger for more spirituality in people's lives.

In one of his talks, he relates the tale of the King Cyrus mentioned in the Bible. This particular king decides to send the Jews back to their homeland to live as Jews once again. Peterson argues that Christians have got to remain Christians even in the overwhelmingly secular West and believe that their values still have worth and significance today.

Personally, I was becoming increasingly attracted to Christian existentialism: the notion that God needs to be experienced and understood in human terms above all else. 'The glory of God is a fully alive human being', the saying attributed to one of the early Church Fathers, Ireneaus, summed it up for me.

The old top-down model of the minister with a monopoly of wisdom and the audience sitting there passively listening was just not viable any more. Part of Peterson's success was the inter-active element he encouraged in his talks, asking questions and encouraging response from his audience. I also wanted to see a more interactive, conversational church experience.

I read about Nikolai Berdayev, the Russian Christian Existentialist and his idea of an 'eighth day of creation', where human kind can work together with God to create something completely new and radical. I like that idea of a joint enterprise between God and humanity.

May 5th 2018
The logo is accepted at the Steering Committee at Y Morlan. Everybody feels happy about it. There's none of the

reservations that came to light with the choice of Ein Gwlad as a name. It feels as if we are finally getting somewhere.

Our collaborative approach seems so right somehow. I find a quote by the newly formed Engage party in England, who also want to pursue a more participative political course: "*The collective thoughts of the many are preferable to the selective opinions of the few*". It seems to be the very thing that Ein Gwlad are all about.

I'm like a magpie like that. I love picking things up from all kinds of different directions and then filing them away in my own little nest in my head. These can fly like a bird when the occasion calls for it.

One of the practices I've adopted over the past few years is to keep a gratitude journal. There's a growing body of scientific evidence which says that gratitude is one of the very best things you can do for your mental and emotional health in life.

Experts say that expressing gratitude can actually change the molecular structure of the brain, and boost the feel-good chemicals, serontonin and dopamine. My practice amounts to jotting down at least ten things I'm grateful for in my life every single day and review the list before going to sleep each night. It's a good way also to write down encouraging, inspirational and informational quotes from different places.

It's also very gratifying on another level to find modern scientific validation for something which is such an integral art of the faith tradition. As the Christian Mystic Meister Eckart put it back in the middle ages,

"If the only prayer you ever say in your life is thank you, it will be enough".

As Steering Committee members we are also all very thankful for the final design drawn up by Mike Murphy's designer friend. Mike reckons it beats all the logos of all the other political parties in Wales hands down.

We have a new member on the Steering Committee. Rhydian Hughes, from Pentrefoelas, a huge bear of a man who used to be an amateur boxer. Rhydian is currently the Vice-Chair of YES Cymru, so he is a very useful member to have on board. He runs a school of motoring in the north, and he is passionate and dedicated. He happens to have a Polish wife and he has travelled extensively in Poland and the east.

Funnily enough, we also find that Stephen Morris has a Polish wife, and will in due course write another article for nation.cymru taking a look at modern Poland and considering the lessons that this country has for Wales. We're becoming Internationalist in our outlook.

Rhydian, having travelled extensively in the old eastern Europe believes that a lot of these new nations, such as Slovenia, Slovakia, Croatia have a lot to teach Wales in the way that they have managed to transform their economies after escaping the clutches of communism.

He tells us that he is concerned about the socialist elements which are emerging within YES Cymru, which he feels are endangering the notion of being a broad church to campaign for independence without being in thrall to any one particular ideology. There's talk of one particular YES Cymru group asking new recruits to sign up to some 'socialist manifesto' before being able to join.

This particular concern is to come to a head within YES Cymru within a very short time.

This is a good time for Big Gee to flesh out his vision of Syncretic Politics. Nobody within the group is quite sure what Gwilym has in mind with 'Syncretic politics'. We're like the disciples in the Bible sometimes, very slow to catch on to what our leader has in mind. But, once he gets in his stride, to explain it is has an immediate appeal.

He prepares a paper: 'Syncretism- a combination of separate concepts into one new, unique idea.'

"Instead of following a particular political ideology, or dogma, one may identify strengths and weaknesses in many of them and try to absorb those which appear positive and simultaneously discard those that seem negative (for example pure socialism or stats). Simply put, syncretic politics are not 'left' or 'right' but what is right or wrong for my country). When asked if Ein Gwlad is right or left, we simply reply that "we are Welsh". Our only focus is what's best for Wales and its people. We do not subscribe to right wing, centralist or left wing (abstract, outdated and defunct) concepts of traditional politics. That single axis paradigm is a thing of the past."

He goes on to mention that syncretic parties are springing up all over Europe, disparaged constantly by the conventional media as 'populists'.

Gee refers to the Oxford Dictionary definition of 'populist':

'A political approach that strives to appeal to ordinary people who feel their concerns are disregarded by established elite groups.'

And

'The practice of policies aimed at ordinary people'.

He writes that, quite simply, a syncretic party is one which does not align itself to any particular position on the ideological spectrum, either on the left or the right. It focuses rather on pragmatic politics, what's right for the particular situation in question. He refers to a Syncretic Bulgarian party- which says, "We're not left, nor right- we're Bulgarian".

Gwyn then comes up with a handy line to be used: "We're not left, we're not right- we are straight-forward", which I like a lot.

The slogan is later to be honed to read, "We are not left or right - just Welsh."

A month or so earlier, the populists had triumphed at the Italian Elections. A new coalition was subsequently set up between the Five Star Movement – Originally led by a comic (there's a lesson there somewhere) - and the Northern League, with both parties opposed to the European Union and seeking to re-establish Italian sovereignty.

The two parties found overwhelming support from the Italian public fed up of the EU's continual austerity agenda and its open doors migration policy, which had seen thousands upon thousands of African migrants turning up on Italy's shores. The sheer scale of the migration was hard enough for many Italians to accept, but a resulting crimewave amongst the arrivals in many small towns and villages along the Italian coast proved the final straw for many.

The new government devised a syncretic approach to policy-making with their promises including a Citizen's Income and a new tough migration policy to appeal to as many Italians as possible.

Over the next few months, 'Populism' continued to be demonized at every opportunity by the political elite/media. But, to more and more people, populism appeared to be a completely rational and democratic response to the arrogant Liberal Technocracy who seemed to think 'there is no alternative' to their world view. People all over Europe were increasingly saying no their elites and looking for new vehicles to represent their interests.

A huge Ipsos Mori Poll in 2017 which quizzed 18,000 people across 25 European nations showed the way the tide was flowing. Respondents provided overwhelming support for the statement "Traditional parties and politicians don't care about me", with this figure reaching 67% in France and 65% of respondents in the UK. The writing was surely on the wall; for all who wanted to see. But yet later that summer, a prominent MEP will propose that the EU spend a billion Euros promoting 'union values' to keep the show on the road. People who were voting in their millions for parties wanting to chart a new course for their individual countries, were now being told that their own money would be spent to persuade them otherwise. You just couldn't make all this up.

The European Union's master plan to dissolve national identities and create one European Super state was being exposed as never before as the fanaticism of the centre and something to be resisted at all cost. A renewed emphasis on national borders, identity, culture and belonging were surely going to be the dominant themes over the next few years.

Ein Gwlad seems to be in the right place at the right time. And syncretism could be the key to it all to appeal to as many people as possible in different parts of the country.

But, Wales being Wales, the rumour mill is going into overdrive and the arrival of the new 'right wing' party is being pushed within the media and other circles.

I try the syncretic argument on Big D. "So, you are not going to be right wing b...... after all" he says, with a wink. Maybe I can convert him after all...!

May 12th 2018
We are six months into the project. I've found myself becoming more and more involved despite my initial wariness. I find myself enjoying the discussions both on the steering committee and the forums, and I suppose I am developing a growing confidence that I have a contribution to make.

And hell - I like these guys, warts and all! I enjoy working alongside them. I want this to work!

But as someone who can sometimes allow his enthusiasm for causes to run ahead of itself, I decide I need to give myself a reality check. "Check your thoughts every now and then," says Big D. It's good advice.

I decide to draw up a balance-sheet listing all the obstacles that Ein Gwlad will face allied to some of the possibilities and opportunities that have emerged.

OBSTACLES:

*Wales has been annexed by England for almost five centuries, from 1536. That's quite a long time really.

*The vote for the national party, Plaid Cymru, in existence for almost a century, is a meagre 20% at best.

* Wales's economy is highly integrated economically with England, and fresh moves afoot to link the north into a Mersey super region and the south into a Bristol super region.

* Wales has a national deficit of some £14 billion (the difference between the amount spent here by the UK government and the taxes raised here)

* 20% of the population of Wales were born in England. In some places along the north wales coast this is closer to 40%.

*Wales is served by an overwhelmingly English based media. The highest selling newspaper in Wales is the odious Daily Mail (apparently a 100,000 copies a day). The Welsh media is tiny and insignificant with most papers under the control of Trinity Holdings, again an entity which is based over the border. Most of the Welsh population therefore is fed a daily diet of English-based propaganda where a Welsh perspective on things is completely missing.

* In the Brexit Referendum vote, Wales's voting pattern mimicked England's voting pattern almost to a tee, around 52% to 48% for Leave. Some were even saying that a new entity was now in place, after that referendum, Wangland. Especially as Scotland and Northern Ireland had voted to stay in the EU - Scotland by a very decisive margin of 62% to 38%.

* The Welsh people seemed in general to be caught in a death-spiral of negativity, hopelessness, despair and lack of confidence.

*Politicians and political parties in general were despised. Was another political party likely to change those perceptions??!!

It's quite a long list. I could have added to it easily, but I decide that's quite enough of a reality check for the time being.

So what could go on the other side of the balance sheet? I need to think about this for a while.

OPPORTUNITIES:

*The enduring sense of strong Welsh identity. In a recent survey, nearly 60% of the Welsh population still think of themselves as primarily Welsh. 20% thought of themselves as primarily British, and 20% thought of themselves as primarily English. That's encouraging for a start.

* The Brexit Referendum. Even though Wales had voted the same way as England, Brexit was still a huge catalyst for change here. Nothing could ever be the same after Brexit. This opened up the possibility of more and more people responding to new ideas.

* That £14 billion deficit could easily be trimmed .After all an Independent Wales is hardly likely to want to spend 4% of its budget on Defence like the UK who still have delusions about being a big player on the world stage. Following the Irish model of spending 2% on defence would bring the Welsh deficit down to £12 billion. We would no longer be paying towards UK projects like Crossrail, HS2 and other London vanity projects. That's another £1b slashed off the deficit. Down to around £11 billion. Just to start. And anyway, almost every nation on earth runs a budget deficit.

* Change was happening all over Europe at this point in time. Brexit was being replicated in many other countries

in various ways: In Italy, Austria, Germany and in the Visegrad Bloc of nations (Hungary, Poland, Czech Republic and Slovakia) there seemed to a big clamour for change and new parties appearing promising to prioritise the needs of ordinary people over the Liberal European elite who have ruled the roost for so long. Ein Gwlad could be part of this new wave.

* The European Soccer Championships of 2016. That summer of Welsh footballing success, with the national team reaching the semi-finals against Portugal was a very joyous time to be Welsh. Wales was being represented on the world stage at long last. Those summer weeks seemed to bring the Welsh nation together - both Welsh-speaking and English-speaking - north, east, west, south, in a way that had never happened before.

The Welsh fans who went out to France were magnificent, winning praise and admiration from all quarters for their support for the team and their good behaviour all round. Wales had not only had a world stage that summer, they had managed to forge a world-wide profile during that hazy July month in 2016. That quarter-final tie when we had defeated Belgium 3-1 with their multi-talented squad of players, was just an unbelievable night for all concerned.

If the Brexit vote had seemed to extinguish Wales as a distinct nation a couple of months previously, our soccer team had almost single-handedly revived that identity overnight. Those proud patriotic feelings were not going to go away. Someone or other could surely tap into these feelings on a political level.

* The existence of our national language. Yes, it's seen as divisive by some, and with only 20% of the population speaking Welsh at present, it could easily be termed an obstacle to any hopes of Welsh Independence. But, with a recent survey showing that 81% of the people of Wales

were supportive of the language and 63% saying they would like to learn Welsh: the very presence of the language, the identity it provides, and its creative power can be a huge advantage for the independence movement.

* The growth of Yes Cymru, with new YES groups emerging all over Wales was very encouraging. The case for independence was finally being made and new people being drawn into their activities and communications. Despite the slightly fractured relationship which would develop between the two organizations over the next few month, YES Cymru was still a really important and significant development.

* Oh, and we've got world-beater Geraint Thomas as well! A Welsh winner of The Tour De France Titw Thomas, Titw Thomas Las!

I feel that reality check has been a worthwhile exercise. The balance sheet is clearly still more weighed towards the obstacles. The odds are still heavily stacked against us, but don't all of us need challenges in life?!

May 20, 2018

I take my parents on a long-awaited week's vacation to Aberystwyth. A glorious week of weather is promised, and it is duly delivered.

One of the perks of working for the Presbyterian Church of Wales is Ty Barclay, in Aberystwyth. Ty Barclay is a house situated near the promenade, which is kept for the use of staff members and their families - bequeathed by a former minister, Barclay Griffiths. My mate, Tim Hodgins from Port Talbot first alerted me to this opportunity for a free holiday in

Aberystwyth, and this is the second such holiday I have taken there.

Ty Barclay is a bit of an oddity to say the least. The lounge and bedrooms seem to have been preserved in aspic since the 1950ies, but this is counterposed with a spanking new kitchen, which I know my mother will enjoy pottering about in .

My parents have hours of innocent fun going through a comments book which has been completed by all the other guests and families who have stayed at Ty Barclay over the years. The names of people they have known over the years trip off the tongue. It's a like a Who's Who of the Presbyterian Church of Wales.

My favourite contribution to the well-leafed comments book has been left by someone with a wicked sense of humour.

'Many thanks to the Connexion for their kind hospitality during a particularly trying and stressful time in my life, when I was trying to rehabilitate myself'. Yours Sincerely, Ronald Biggs.

The use of the word Connexion (another name for the PCW) seems particularly apt with its connotations of some shadowy, underworld movement which would want to give succour to a master criminal such as Ronnie Biggs! Well, Gwyn did suggest that I could become a shadowy figure, so perhaps I am in the right place after all!

I have a tiny room at the front of the house, but I'm not bothered by this at all since I can hear the waves breaking on the seafront last thing at night and first thing in the morning. Heaven.

My father, who himself has recovered from a long bout of illness, has found a new lease of life in his early 80s. We vie for the honour of the first to rise for an early morning walk around Aberystwyth before breakfast. It's a glorious time to be up and about. The day is full of promise.

My Dad who has been a huge influence in my life, is really funny sometimes. He can't fathom how I can cope without a wife and a family life to sustain me, but he's managed to come to terms with it somehow.

So has my Mam, a more reserved individual than my father, but perhaps an even greater influence on me in her own way. Secretly, I think she's glad to still have an opportunity to fuss over me.

She prepares breakfast for us whilst my Dad and I go on our early morning walks. We swap anecdotes about family experiences over the years and I remind him of that story when I went to see our family doctor Dr. John Hughes who was a real character, with a pain in my ankle.

"Oh, you poor boy, another of your father's heavy sermons has fallen on your foot again!", he said with a pained expression on his face. You never knew with Dr Hughes if he was being serious or not.

I'm very attached to Gwynedd, since I really appreciate the fact that I can mostly live my life naturally through the medium of Welsh there. But if I had to choose another place to live in Wales, it would definitely be Aberystwyth. There's an airiness and lightness to the seaside town which is beyond words somehow.

The irony is I'm much more fond of the place now than when I was a student here all those years ago. Most people have an irrational attachment to their student days seeing them as the best days of their lives, where the best and closest friendships in life are formed. It's typical of me that I find a new love for Aberystwyth long after my student days. And that I have made some of my own most meaningful friendships well after that period as well.

My parents and I have enjoyed long leisurely days walking the prom and enjoying meals in the different cafes and restaurants in Aberystwyth. One particular highlight is a visit to 'Pysgoty' (the fish house), which is a new restaurant on the far end of the prom at Aberystwyth. I have monkfish to eat. It's probably the tastiest meal I have had for years.

My Dad insists on playing for our meals. I tease him, it's only fair bearing in mind that I have paid for the hotel! Hat-tip to the Presbyterian Church of Wales!

It's great to be able to have a holiday of this nature with my parents. It's maybe one of the benefits of being single - that one does tend to have a closer relationship with your parents than would be the case if one was married.

After being in a series of relationships over the years, I have been single for the past two years. For a red-blooded Welshman, there are obvious disadvantages of course. But, I have genuinely embraced singledom at this point in my life. I'm learning to appreciate all the freedoms of being single. Of being independent. Latest figures show that almost 40% of the people of Wales are now single. It's not as if I am all alone in this respect.

I think the best part of being single for some time is to know that one can manage and cope with life alone. Should I ever find another relationship, I will have no fear about that coming to an end, since I know that I can manage on my own.

It's a whole new way of relating, I find. I like the fact that, being single, I can maintain a connection to many people on different levels. I like being my own man. I Like being independent. I'm glad I don't have to battle to keep up a sense of status and social standing that so many married couple seem to be engaged in these days. "Marriage is a great institution" quipped Groucho Marx. "But who wants to live in an institution!"

It also of course, gives me an opportunity to devote some time to an enterprise like Ein Gwlad. If I was married, I would have probably been warned off getting involved in such a madcap venture.

Is Ein Gwlad indeed a substitute for the missing love interest in my life?

May 23rd 2018

I pop over to Llanddeiniol, outside Aberystwyth to see Gwyn. I must have passed by on that road hundreds of times over the years - but this is the very first time I've been to Llanddeiniol, a mile or so from the main road. One of my crazy ambitions is to visit every village and town in Wales during my lifetime- and now I've managed to cross another one off my list. It's still quite a long list mind.

Gwyn lives at Benglog, a working farm at the furthest end of Llanddeiniol. I also meet his wife, Ingrid, who is an Austrian whom Gwyn met during his career in textiles. Ingrid's done her best to learn Welsh since moving to Wales he says, but the mutations were too problematical for her as a methodical German speaker. She's also quite an accomplished painter with some of her work adorning the walls of their home.

Gwyn serves us some tea and I sit back waiting for some more bullish tales from his business experiences over the years.

But, he tells me that he is on his way to Aberystwyth that afternoon to do some counselling work with CRUSE (the charity that offers support for bereaved individuals). He's done this work voluntarily for some twenty years. I also find out that he spent ten years working with SEREN - a charity which works with adults who have been sexually abused during their childhood. There's a strong social conscience there beneath the bullish exterior. And a great sense of humour as well.

Somehow, I manage to lose my sunglasses in his house, even though I've only been in the kitchen and bathroom. Both of us rummage around for a good five minutes, but they have somehow disappeared into thin air.

Later on that evening, he sends me a picture of the sunglasses perched on a white dressing gown in the bathroom.

Both of us had failed to spot them, even though they were hiding in full sight.

'Should have gone to Specsavers!' is the message underneath.

May 25th 2018

The YES CYMRU Caernarfon group meet in the town's Galeri centre. Last year's National Eisteddfod crown winner, Gwion Hallam chairs the meeting. Gwion has been the driving force of YES Caernarfon since its inception a year ago. He somehow manages to balance all the organisational work of keeping members in the loop about things with his everyday work as a television producer and being the father of four boys.

The group have been asked to discuss a 'Declaration of Independence' statement prepared by YES CYMRU's central committee. Iwan Rhys, who represents YES Caernarfon on that committee tells the group that the intention is for it to be the equivalent of The Irish Declaration of Independence in 1916 and the America Declaration of Independence in 1776.

Iwan somehow manages to keep a straight face in telling us this, but I can tell that even he thinks it's a load of old bull.

Apparently, this 'Declaration of Independence' is to be released to the media in a few weeks' time, but all the different groups in Wales are being invited to submit their comments as part of a brief consultative process. We're told we have to get our comments in by the end of the week. It's Wednesday night now. How keen are they to get comments with such a tight deadline?

YES Cymru have been making great strides of late with new groups being set up in different parts of Wales. But it seems to me that this progress has gone to their heads entirely. A Declaration of Independence! What on earth are they smoking down at that central committee in Cardiff?!!

It's laughable that they could ever think to compare the paltry efforts made here for Independence for Wales over the years to the years of struggle, sacrifice and bloodletting which eventually led to the respective declaration of independence in both Ireland and America.

The statement itself is full of banalities about the huge struggles of working people in Wales over the centuries, and that now is the time to throw off the shackles of Westminster and embrace Independence at long last. It reads like an essay prepared by an over-excited sixth former trying to impress his form teacher.

Worse, it completely contradicts YES Cymru's over-arching aim of trying to be as broad a church as possible in presenting the case for independence to the people of Wales. The flowery language of the statement can't disguise the fact that this is a socialist take on the meaning of Independence for Wales. This socialist leaning amongst some members of the central committee was to lead to serious misgivings amongst others within the ranks and lead to something of an internal revolt later that summer.

There seems to be a consensus amongst the members of YES Caernarfon that the statement is much too premature and needs to be withdrawn. We agree to send in our comments to the YES Cymru central committee. This opinion is seemingly shared by other groups and the 'Declaration of Independence' is shelved for the time being. Although we are told that the work has now been delegated to the YES London group for some reason.

The whole issue is a salutary lesson on how NOT to do things. It also perhaps suggests some immaturity and hot-headedness within the leadership of YES Cymru. Big Gee's insistence on taking our time and preparing the ground properly before launching Ein Gwlad seems to be vindicated even more after this particular episode.

As the Chairperson, he has always argued that anticipation about our arrival has got to be built up gradually over a number of months, and that we should beware of striking too soon. The saying, 'Fools rush in where Angels dare to tread' comes to mind.

We may be middle-aged and wrinkly as a Steering Group- but perhaps there are advantages associated with our advancing years after all.

PEN PORTRAIT 7

Darren Owen.
Born in Caerffili. Living in Caerffili.

I have known for as long as I can remember that Cymru has suffered great injustice at the hands of the 'British' establishment. My own Grandmother was sent off, like many a Cymraes,(aged 14),to "do service" i.e. be a servant, to a rich lady in London. She got married there, and if she hadn't divorced,(frowned upon at the time),returned home and re-united with my Grandfather, I would not be here typing this.

We were still allowed our own English language Welsh TV programmes when I was young,(if you lived in the right part of town),and there was truth in these that showed further the way things have been for the Cymru at the hands of the establishment.

I have lived in the Valleys all my life and seen first-hand the situations caused by uncaring politicians who look after only themselves. I've seen neighbour turned against neighbour, brother against brother over games played by the establishment. They caused an horrendous situation then left the Valleys for dead. Not a nice place to grow up. The people responsible would do the same thing again tomorrow without even thinking about it. Parasites like these are something Cymru does not and never did need.

The Welsh People just need to see through their (sometimes clever) lies. Labour as unionists are part of this establishment and have been leading the Valleys a merry dance for a long, long time.

The more I learned about the abuse Cymru has suffered the more horrified I have become. We are denied our own history and media and so do not know anything other than that which the establishment wants.

Cymru would never have been a country in the first place if we had wanted to be anything other than 'Welsh'. I believe as a Nation we deserve nothing but the best, after what we have had to put up with, what Cymru has had to put up with.

Ideology in the political left/right/centre way has no place in matters pertaining to Cymru's freedom. Cymru's culture is not only my culture, but the culture of my ancestors and my descendants. That of my family, friends and my Nation. It is our very identity at stake.

Cymru deserves to be the happiest Nation on Earth. I want the Hwyl of the Red Wall, so strong we could feel it in my town from France, happiness, contentment. I don't want an independent Wales where you basically can't say anything for fear of possibly offending somebody with a perfectly innocent comment. That is not freedom.

When Ein Gwlad was conceived I was overjoyed as by this time I had nobody to vote for. I don't know a lot about politics,(I don't need to, the politicians are meant to serve the people rather than the other way around)so I offered my services and ended up getting the Facebook side of things going.

Simple work - spread the word so as not to rely on the MSM and post that I'm given. Not rocket science, but stuff that needed doing and which would also allow more time for those with all the political experience to organise everything for the launch of the Party. I'm pleased to have been part of the whole process and pleased to be part of a party that truly wants what's best for Cymru - unconditionally.

June 2nd 2018

However positive Ein Gwlad aims to be with a focus on our particular mission above all else, it's inevitable that the failings of Plaid Cymru as the established national party have to be addressed. I'm a bit wary in this respect, because it's a slightly sensitive subject for me personally.

I was in a relationship for six years with Sian Gwenllian, who is now the Plaid AM for Arfon. Wales is a small place and there's always the possibility that some will say that there's some personal grievance in place in becoming part of a new party, which like it or not is going to be seen as a full-frontal challenge to Plaid Cymru. But this isn't personal.

Sian is a wonderful individual, who helped me a lot at quite a difficult time in my personal life. She's a dedicated and hard-working politician who really is well-grounded in her community.No, this is political.

Plaid in my humble opinion have lost their way completely over a number of years. The loss of 1,000 members over the past year alone speaks volumes.

As a party they do have some very articulate and talented individuals in their ranks. The two Westminster MP's, Jonathan Edwards and Liz Saville Roberts (a former work colleague of mine) being two prime examples of that. But, collectively, they just don't seem to be a coherent party with a clear and understandable message for the public at all.

The truth is that the rot set in many years ago.

It might have taken place a good few years ago, but the decision of MP Dafydd Ellis Thomas to accept a Lordship to the House of Lords was an indicator of things to come. The membership of course voted clearly against this fundamental change of party policy. But the MP was given special dispensation to have his own way. Lord Ellis Thomas has always seemed to enjoy flaunting his Lordship for some reason.

And recently, another former MP, Dafydd Wigley decided to join him in the House of Lords. The membership once again was left to fume in silence and frustration at yet another policy betrayal. This time by Dafydd Wigley. And he was supposed to be the good Dafydd!

The SNP in Scotland have always retained their core principle of not sending members to the House of Lords. That consistency seems to have paid off for them. Voters just don't like or respect parties that break their key promises. Just look at what happened to the Lib Dems after they broke their promises on tuition fees.

Plaid have always shied away from truly promoting independence for Wales, using the pretext of regular opinion polls over the years that showed the support for Welsh Independence at no more than 10 per cent. But then, with not even Wales's own national party putting the case for independence, how on earth was that figure ever going to increase? The party's inherent cautiousness and circumspection concerning the very raison d'etre of the Welsh national cause was a long-standing source of dissatisfaction for many of their own supporters.

Then there is their complete inconsistency concerning nuclear power. Plaid Cymru has had a policy of opposing nuclear power, faithfully maintained by their members at conferences year in, year out. Yet, the party leadership have been in favour of a new nuclear station to be built on Ynys Mon - to meet the energy demands of England - because this was a 'special case'. The special case being that they had an AM representing the island.

AM Rhun ap Iorwerth's favourite line, trotted out at every possibility:

"How can I look Carwyn from Llangristiolus (a small village where both he and Carwyn live) in the eye, and say that I oppose Wylfa B, when's he hoping to find work there?" struck me as being the worse type of barrel-pump politics.

It just gave the impression that the MP was in it for the status and the power alone and was willing to spout a folk-spun homily - which became more embarrassing every single time he repeated it - to try and justify the unjustifiable.

This nuclear issue was to haunt Rhun ap Iorwerth when he contended for the Plaid leadership later that year.

Leanne Wood's leadership for the past six years has also seen Plaid pursue a socialist and 'progressive' agenda, where every noble cause under the sun seems to be just as important as Wales itself. Leanne herself of course had maybe more publicity than any previous Plaid leader, featuring in public debates at the time of the referendum and in the general election over the past few years. Her core support thought she did wonderfully. But Plaid's vote remained static despite all the plaudits.

It struck me as very telling that her two most memorable contributions during those debates were 'progressive' put-downs for UKIP's Nigel Farage and his successor, the hapless Paul Nuttall. The Guardian and the Liberal Left of course lapped these up. But they were nothing at all to do with the Welsh National Interest. The very USP of our national party.

More locally in Gwynedd and Ynys Mon, the party's policy of closing rural schools in favour of new 'super-schools' seemed to fly in the face of everything the party had ever stood for, supporting and sustaining local communities. This policy might have pleased their Labour overlords at the Assembly, but it just managed to completely alienate a lot of their core support. This has allowed a small and completely fractious group, Llais Gwynedd to win many council seats from Plaid Cymru over recent years.

But the last straw for me personally, which led me to give up my post of secretary of a local branch and resign my membership entirely took place last year. This was when the Plaid group on Cyngor Gwynedd decided to back a Local Development Plan to build up to 8,000 houses on Ynys Mon and Gwynedd between 2015-2025. There is no way at all that these houses are to meet local need.

It was an LDP foisted on Welsh councils by the Planning Inspectorate in London. A good few Plaid councillors did in fairness do their best to oppose the LDP, but at the decisive meeting the casting vote of the Plaid Chairman meant the LDP was passed.

Being present at that council debate was a depressing affair, hearing so many of Plaid's senior Cabinet Members arguing in favour of the 8,000 houses. It proved once again that many of Plaid Cymru's representatives now saw themselves as 'Managers' not 'Politicians', eager to please and ingratiate themselves with council functionaries, rather than challenge and fight against a plan imposed from London. Their line, *"Look, trust us - we're Plaid Cymru"*, when that trust has long disappeared, was a further indication to many of how much they have the lost the plot.

The LDP issue was fast becoming a national issue, as a similar plan to foist 40,000 new homes in the capital city Cardiff was also met with a wave of local protests, with a series of packed-out meetings over the summer of 2018 voicing concerns about the loss of green field sites, fears of pollution and congestion and increased pressures on local health services with such a massive influx of new residents.

But there was also a deeper problem at work beyond individual policy issues within Wales's national party. It seemed to me that Plaid Cymru had become a party dedicated solely to the business of 'getting someone in', be that to the Assembly or Westminster every 4/5 years, and that the whole party machinery was devoted to this aim. Beyond these feverish bouts of activity, there was nothing. Zilch. Nada. Dim byd.

There was no real attempt to educate and agitate for the national cause amongst the Welsh population and try and bring more people into the national movement. As long as a few choice individuals were elected every few years to these elevated positions at Cardiff Bay or Westminster, the party seemed satisfied.

On my home island of Ynys Mon, the party's branches are practically moribund, staging a few coffee mornings here and there, peopled mainly by older members. There is no political culture there at all. Over the water in Arfon, another safe Plaid seat, it is more or less the same tale.

Devolution seems to have drained all the vitality out of Plaid Cymru. What remains now is a husk of a party, staggering on just in order to justify its own existence, but going nowhere in truth. If Plaid Cymru were an animal, surely a humane vet would have decided to end its sufferings by now.

June 9th 2018

Gruff Meredith, who made an appearance at the initial meeting at Aberystwyth, gets in touch to say that he would like to run an article about Ein Gwlad for Y Cymru's special Eisteddfod edition at the start of August. Griff is now the editor of Y Cymro.

At the Steering Committee, we agree to accept his invitation, and again, we decide it is to be a collaborative process between our members. Gwyn Wigley Evans and I decide we will work together to write it by use of Google Docs.

The articles which have appeared so far about Ein Gwlad have been quite diffuse. And maybe not direct enough if truth be told. Gwyn and I decide to take a different approach with this article and compose it in the form of a number of questions and answers.

We also think this will be a means of answering some of the objections that were raised in the first article written by Stephen Morris.

I take the lead with Gwyn adding to the material as we progress. Big Gee also casts his beady eye over the article before it is sent on to the editor.

Both suggest that the tone is too conciliatory. Both Gwyn and Gwilym think the article should be more assertive and really go for the jugular as far as Plaid Cymru are concerned. i.e. that Ein Gwlad is a direct result of the fact that Plaid Cymru have proved to be such a let-down for so many years.

Perhaps they have a point. I just feel that it is important not to be seen to be too negative and condemnatory at the outset. I make the point that there no need to really spell out all Plaid's failings since people know all too well what those failings are as it is.

I think it's better to focus on all the positives associated with a new political party, especially in this particular period of time. I say we can always be more assertive if the need arises in future. For now, a 'softly-softly' approach is better. To my surprise, they agree, if slightly grudgingly.

I'm glad that I have stood my ground against the two Alpha Males of Ein Gwlad. Who knows, maybe I can learn to become one myself. Alpha Males have had a bad press over the years, being associated with a range of negative behaviours both in a personal sense and a social/political sense.

I've never wanted to be associated with all that. But, I've read about a new definition of an Alpha Male. This gives it a much more positive spin than the way it has been portrayed traditionally.

-embrace your flaws
-approve of yourself
-find brotherhood
-don't be afraid to rock the boat
-chase your dream

Maybe these traits are just what I need to develop in myself.

Maybe these traits can also be put to good use in a wider sense as well.

Even so, I ask Gwyn if he's ok to be identified as the author of the article. I've got my reasons for not penning my name to it, but Gwyn, fair play to him doesn't pry into those reasons and says he's willing for his name to be on it.

I'm not entirely clear in my own mind why that should be the case, but I know instinctively that I don't want to be named at this point. Maybe it's the introversion. Not quite the Alpha Male just yet.

Some of the questions and answers for Y Cymro article.

Why establish Ein Gwlad at this particular point?

It's an exciting period of change everywhere at present. Here in the UK for example - Brexit has changed everything. But change is happening across Europe at the moment, as people in several countries express their dissatisfaction with the present state of affair, the present political parties. People are waking up and voting for new and fresh political parties. Ein Gwlad are part of this new movement and as part of this, we have to be much more assertive and direct in standing up for Wales and her people.

We cannot accept one blow after the other in such a passive manner any more - a nuclear power station being imposed upon us, even though we are well able to meet our own energy requirements; powers being drawn back to London from our National Assembly; a world leading tidal energy scheme for Swansea Bay rejected by Westminster; The Severn Bridge renamed the Prince of Wales bridge in a totally underhand and undemocratic manner etc, etc. This in addition to the old familiar problems, poverty, poor levels of health, lack of work and investment, our public services being decimated and the decline of our national language and culture. And above all else - the sheer sense of despair and hopelessness to be seen throughout our communities, throughout Wales.

We need to transform everything in every sense if the country we love so much is to reach its potential. We believe that Wales could become the best small country in the world to live in - if she is free to make her own decisions. That's the country Ein Gwlad wants to see and that's why we have formed."

The second question agreed sought to address the most obvious objections that people would have to a new party. Some of the objections we had heard already.
Wales has one national party already. Won't you just be splitting the vote by competing with Plaid Cymru?

"With only one party saying they are for independence in Wales - often in a mealy-mouthed way - anyone who wants to see independence has to vote for all that party's policies, even though they may not approve of all of them. With more than one party arguing for independence, we can move the debate onwards from the question, 'should we be independent?' to 'what kind of independent country we want to be?' - and offer a wider choice for people. Countries similar to Wales, such as the Basque County and Catalunya both have three to five national parties each which can attract votes from different directions aiming for the same objective. That's the model we should emulate in Wales. Plaid Cymru's core vote is around 20%.That leaves 80% of the Welsh population we can appeal to."

The next section mentioned the more conciliatory approach that had eventually been agreed by the Steering Committee:
"We believe we need to co-operate extensively with others to win freedom for Wales. That means we are willing to co-operate with Plaid Cymru and the other parties that are willing to work towards this aim. Working alongside other groups such as Yes Cymru will also be essential in this respect. We have to work together. Let us remember the old saying, 'Strength in Union'.

It is quite possible that Scotland will gain its own independence by 2021. In such circumstances, the election to the Welsh Assembly in 2021 will be totally different; Ein Gwlad will be in a good place to take advantage.

The next question was an opportunity to flesh out Big Gee's big idea, Syncretism.

You describe yourself as a 'syncretic' party. What does that mean to the man on the street?

"In stating that Ein Gwlad will be a syncretic party, we are rejecting the tired and increasingly irrelevant model which has typified the politics of these isles for so long. Ein Gwlad will not be a party on 'the left', not a party 'on the right' nor a party 'in the centre'. Rather EG will be a Welsh party, placing the interests of Wales and its people above any ideological 'baggage' or one-party political dogma. We will provide pragmatic answers to the requirements of Wales in this period and to the future - without being bound to the restrictive and divisive party dogma of the past.

We believe that Wales' size and the social capital which is so strong throughout our Welsh speaking and English communities alike makes it an ideal location for a new syncretic politics."

The next question addresses the issue of Yes Cymru, the organisation which had garnered so much support of late.

The non-party aligned movement, YES Cymru, has a good deal of momentum at present. Wouldn't it be better for you to join up with them?

"We welcome the great steps that YES Cymru have taken over the past eighteen months. They have managed to convey the message about independence in a vibrant and imaginative fashion to a brand-new audience here in Wales. As mentioned previously, we intend to work closely with YES Cymru. Many of our registered members are also members of different YES Cymru groups all over Wales, therefore this dialogue has started already!

The difference is of course that Ein Gwlad will be standing in elections to the Welsh Senedd - something that YC do not intend to do. Although we acknowledge the importance of raising awareness about independence in our communities and putting pressure on the other parties, we believe we must win political power for ourselves through the ballot box to achieve his aim. We can't just rely on the other parties in this respect."

There was no avoiding the big issue of the day, Brexit. We wanted to come across as pragmatic, and positive if possible.

Where do you stand on the big issue of our period, Brexit? Are there any new opportunities for Wales as part of this process at all?

"Quite simply, the decision concerning Brexit has been taken. There's nothing we can do about this. The UK will leave the European Union at the end of March 2019 - that is the reality. We have no interest in re-fighting the battles of the past in this matter. All we can do is respond to what is now in front of us - offering creative and rational answers to whatever situations Wales will face after leaving the European Union. We appreciate that many people have concerns about Wales' situation outside the EU as regards commerce and exports. All we say is that trade has always been a crucial component in human existence and trade will continue between individuals and countries - whatever any group of politicians decide.

We have to remember that we have our own market of three million people here in Wales and a huge market of nearly sixty million people in England on our doorstep - whatever new arrangements appear with Europe and the wider world. With some imagination and application, a new Welsh economy can be developed which is suitable for our new circumstances."

After answering all the questions, the logical endpoint was to encourage readers to actually join the party and provide reasons why they should do so.

Why should people join up with Ein Gwlad?

"Ein Gwlad's logo is the phoenix raising from the ashes. We believe it sums up our whole vision as a political party, i.e. that Wales rises on its feet as a nation once again. And claims its place as a nation in its own right on the world stage, in the same way that two hundred other countries have taken this step since 1945.

If you are unhappy with the way that London treats Wales- join Ein Gwlad

If you are unhappy with the performance of the Labour Government in Y Senedd- join Ein Gwlad

If you wish to see power and wealth shared to all parts of Wales - not just Cardiff - join Ein Gwlad

If you want to see the case for 'Independence for Wales' presented in a strong and uncompromising way- join Ein Gwlad."

At this meeting I finally get to meet Dr Stephen Morris, 'Eos Pengwern,' who attends his first Steering Group meeting. He is a very polite and well-mannered individual, but it soon becomes clear that we have a brilliant mind at work here.

Stephen will become one of the leading figures in the new party I am sure of that.

We have a discussion about adding some additional values to the constitution document. Mention is made of the Alternative Party in Denmark who managed to win 7.5% of the popular vote in a national election in Denmark a couple of years ago, having only been in existence for eighteen months before the election.

Alternativet's alternative approach to politics could certainly be a model to follow. They first identified a set of core values on which their party would be based, on the premise that people are much more likely to identify with values than policies, in an age where so many people are sceptical about politics and politicians in general.

Values trump policies they declared. These values included Transparency, Courage, Humour, and Empathy. Once those value were in place, the party then drew up their policies based on the findings of a number of 'ideas laboratories' arranged all over Denmark where people could attend and discuss different ideas. Apparently, this unconventional approach had drawn thousands of people along to these laboratories.

We agree that this people-centred approach fits in perfectly with what Ein Gwlad are all about. Once again, a valuable and animated discussion between the steering group members. Later on the forum comes up with a set of our own values that we can promote, and that the Welsh people would respond well to. These include:

Radicalism: Radical and pragmatic solutions to the economic and social issues facing contemporary Wales. Evaluating ideas based on whether these ideas will benefit Wales and her people - not according to what they come from or whether so called left wing or right wing. We are a syncretic party that does not recognise the traditional axis, left, centre or right-wing labelling paradigm.

Courage: We shall not flinch from confronting the scale of the problems facing Wales since, only when problems are faced honestly can they be overcome. We shall be open with each other and the nation at large about what needs to be done.

Creativity: Wales is known across the world as a country where words mean everything. We mean to unleash that power for the good of our economy and communities.

Perseverance: The fact that Wales still exists at all in the 21st Century is testament to our ability to fight against all the odds and find a way through.

Brogarwch: The English language lacks a way to fully express the meaning of this word: a love of place, a commitment to our land and people, yet untainted by chauvinism or jingoism.

June 9th 2018

It becomes apparent that the Welsh Labour government have buckled to pressures imposed by Westminster. Up to now the Welsh Government and the Scottish Government had been presenting a common front that the devolved legislatures should be fully consulted before the implementation of Brexit. There was even talk that Cardiff and Edinburgh could refuse to pass the necessary legislation in their respective parliaments.

But it's announced that the Welsh Government have now decided to cede eight key powers back to Westminster for seven years when the UK leaves the EU. Out-going First Minister Carwyn Jones argues that this is a pragmatic measure to ensure consistent cross-border trade in food, product labelling and the like. You could argue that Carwyn Jones's hands were tied in a way as Wales had voted for Brexit.

Even so, it most probably had nothing to do with Wales as such. Rather it was to all to do with the Labour party and the requirements of the Labour Party, where Carwyn Jones seemed to receive all his instructions. It would not look good for Jeremy

Corbyn and his party, if one part of his Labour empire seemed to be resisting Brexit when he was so dependent on Brexit supporters in many 'Leave' areas in Labour's old industrial heartlands. Once again, the Labour party comes first. Not Wales.

Serving the interests of the Labour party was also at the root of the huge growth of the third sector in Wales over the devolution years. This is a relationship that serves to reward Labour supporters with third sector bodies duplicating work that is done by any number of similar organisations, but also, in rural areas where the party has little support. It gives Labour influence and patronage in places where they otherwise wouldn't enjoy it.

The full absurdity of the situation can only be understood by looking into the third sector and realising that many of those now running third sector bodies have been attracted to Wales by the system and keep the wheels turning by also bringing in 'clients' from England.

It seems we have a whole sector made up of bodies dedicated to alleviating poverty or ending homelessness, or whatever the raison d'être might be, and yet all have a vested interest in arguing that the problem is getting worse - otherwise their funding dries up and they're out of a job! Incredibly, there are now no less than forty-eight different Homelessness Organizations in Wales! That's forty-eight different bodies who have an infinite need for more homeless people to care for. Guess where those homeless people come from?!

The benefit for the Labour Party is that 'Poor Wales' can be blamed on the Tories (whether they're in power or not) and keep enough people voting Labour to give the party control of the Assembly and so the patronage continues.

And this system of patronage and cronyism is paid for out the Welsh public purse.

Unfortunately, much of this sails over the general public's heads and Welsh Labour are unchallenged about it. This is mainly due to the fact that Wales is so badly served by the lack of a home-grown media sector, with most people consuming London based newspapers, and completely unaware of what's going on in their own land.

This lack of real scrutiny is a huge problem for Welsh democracy. A recent survey showed that some 40% of the population believed that health and education were still run by Westminster. After almost twenty years of devolution!

Welsh Labour show no desire to improve this situation. Why would they? When it is so useful for them and keeps them in power unchallenged?

This lack of drive to create a better media for Wales and thus a better democracy, is a sign of a wider lack of ambition for Wales. Labour politicians in Wales seem perfectly happy to run Wales as a region of England. No vision. No inspiration. No ambition.

The late First Minister Rhodri Morgan, for all his undoubted qualities, seemed to sum up this Welsh Labour philosophy perfectly. When he asked what was his greatest achievement as First Minister, he answered in all seriousness: "*Getting the Ryder Cup to Wales*".

That small sentence conveyed so much about Welsh Labour's thinking about Wales. Labour think that the only hope for Wales is that it can be a playground for occasional big sporting events such as the Ryder Cup and the Champions League final and so on. That's it.

There's no idea that Wales is a small but historic nation which could achieve so much if only we had politicians who believed that Wales was a nation which had a right to stand alongside every other nation in the world.

June 15ᵗʰ 2018

Stephen Morris pens another article on nation.cymru. This time, he looks at Poland's development since the end of communism in 1989 with some figures to show how it has become the fastest-growing and most successful of all the former communist countries.

Poland has experienced an amazing 226% growth in GDP since 1989, compared to other smaller countries, such as Slovakia 202%, Lithuania 170%.

The comparable figures nearer to home are 146% for the UK as a whole with Wales averaging 125%.The average Pole is today three times wealthier than the average Pole in 1989.

It's a lengthy tome from Stephen this time, quite academic in parts. Maybe, it's not the best to go on the nation.cymru site to be honest. But even so, there are key messages for Wales here.

He makes a distinction between an 'extractive' economy, with a small elite having control over the country's wealth and natural resources and an 'inclusive' society, where power and wealth are more evenly spread through the population, encouraging everyone in society to contribute and raise the level of the whole society. Poland used to be an extractive economy, it is now an inclusive economy, investing heavily in its people.

This is a model which Wales could obviously emulate. This is also a counter to the usual argument that Wales has lost the boat as far as independence is concerned, seeing that our natural slate, iron and coal have all been extracted many years ago. People are the best resource that any country can have, in essence.

Stephen finishes his article by saying that Poland have had seventeen different governments over a 30-year period which has ensured that no political elite has become too entrenched. So, so different to Wales!

"Here in Wales, I worry that our national government is subject to an ingrained groupthink, believing that somehow Wales can build a prosperous and fair economy on socialist principles. No other country has ever done that, certainly not Poland, and Wales is unlikely to be the first," he concludes.

June 18th 2018

I'm on a church leaders' course at Coleg Trefeca, near Brecon for five days. I love going to Trefeca. There's a tranquility and stillness about the place that I find very reassuring. It was home to the 'family,' a kibbutz-type experiment run by one of Wales's main religious leaders in the 18th Century, Howel Harris.

After some resistance from members in the north based on the fact that Trefeca is so far away from the bulk of the membership, it has finally been decided to denote Trefeca as the new training centre for PCW and the building upgraded at last. All the rooms are now En-Suite. I'm glad that Trefeca's position is now secure for the future.

I sometimes have a fancy that I would enjoy taking part in some form of modern communal living in Wales, similar to the old 'family' experiment at Trefeca. But then, I very much doubt whether I could hack being woken at six am. every morning for a hard day's grind on the farm, being constantly harangued by an authoritative Howel Harris type figure, constantly checking on my behaviour and devotion. Maybe that's not one of my best ideas.

The courses are organised by the church's training officer, Delyth Oswy, and once again it does not disappoint. There's a talk on mental health and the church, a workshop on women in the church and a session with a street pastor in Newport.

There's around twelve of us on the course. Some want to go for ordained ministry. I know that I am not called to that. I don't think I could hack having to be nice to people all the time. And I'm too much of a rebel anyway. But, I'm not sure what

I'm called to. I don't think God is too sure either at the moment. Let's hope we can work something out together.

One of the best talks during the week is given by Dr Peter Stevenson the Principal of the Baptist College at Cardiff. He challenges us to consider the question why preaching is much less popular these days.

Rhys Bebb Jones from Lampeter who is on our table suggests that one of the reasons for this is that everybody fancies themselves as preachers on social media nowadays. With everybody preaching at each other through social media every day, who wants to come along on a Sunday to hear another one, he suggests. It's a good point and one I hadn't considered before.

There're some characters on the course who make us all laugh. One of these is Troy Wright, who is black and who comes from Watford originally but is now working with the church alongside some youngsters in Gower. I'll never forget meeting Troy for the first time in the Cardiff office a year or so previously. During that conversation, I tell Troy that I live in Caernarfon.

"Cae..er.nar..fon," he tries to get his tongue around the unfamiliar words. *"Is that an actual place?"* he asks in some bemusement.

I show him where Caernarfon is on the big map of Wales we have in the office.

"How the hell do you get up there man?" he asks me with a look of incredulity on his face. I assure Troy that we do have a train service of sorts in Wales which can take people from one end of the country to the other - albeit with a huge detour through England on the way.

Troy is always good entertainment. On the Wednesday night, we all go out for a meal to the Old Barn, a local restaurant. Troy is sitting by another participant on the course, Elfed Lewis from Trawsfynydd and somehow manages to mistake Elfed's year of birth for his actual age, which makes him 75 rather than 43.

"You look really good for your age," Troy tells Elfed admiringly. Elfed has a good few silver whisps in his hair, but even so he looks miffed that Troy thinks he's thirty years older than he actually is.

The 75-year-old Elfed is a running joke between us for the next couple of days.

Troy takes it in his stride fair play to him, even referring to it during a time of prayer when each one of us prays for the person sitting next to him before we depart at the end of the course. Troy is sitting by Elfed again and gives us all another fit of giggles when he says. *"Lord, look after Elfed. He is 75 and getting on a bit as you know, but do your best with him!"*

All jokes aside, Troy actually delivers one of the best talks during the week to the group in an evening devotion. He's animated, funny and very effective - we're all eating out of his hands by the end.

After the supper some of us go up to play table tennis. Presbyterians have to play as well as pray after all. Tim Hodgins from Port Talbot and I are amongst the most competitive players, and our bouts eventually work out as 4-4.

I insist that I am the moral victor, bearing in mind that Tim has recently installed two table tennis tables in his church at Sandfields in Port Talbot and is thus getting much more practice than I am. The table have actually managed to attract one or two younger individuals to the church, which Tim is planting on Sandfields, in Port Talbot - one of the biggest council estates in Wales.

I get on well with Tim even though there's a 15-year difference between us. We both have a certain cheekiness about us I think. There's also some vulnerability in Tim which I can relate to.

I admire him because he's battled through some serious drug and alcohol misuse for many years to reach a much better place in life. Too often, our churches are full of people who have breezed through life with complete respectability and conventionality. But I think Tim can relate so much better to the so many broken people we have in Wales today because of his own experiences. Alcohol and drug misuse are huge problems in Wales. It's good to know that we have someone in place who can understand people like this. Someone who has walked in their shoes.

I also chat quite a lot to Elfed Lewis (the above mentioned 75-year-old posing as a 43-year-old). Elfed is a really interesting individual, having spent a good decade working in the IT field out in Canada before returning to Wales last year.

I enjoy listening to Elfed because he is an out-of-the box thinker who is willing to look at things in a completely new way. He and I agree that our institution is coming to an end in its present form and that we need to imagine new ways of doing church today.

He refers to a book he has just read 'The Refusal of Work' by a Cardiff Academic. The author argues that there is a huge amount of 'cultural disappointment' concerning work in our modern society, with all the rhetoric of politicians around the importance and the innate moral worth of work in stark contrast to most people's everyday experiences of work today.

He further argues that we need to move away from a 'work ethic' to a 'worthwhile ethic' which can acknowledge and reward people for a wider range of 'work,' from caring for family, volunteering, political engagement, creativity etc, etc. It's a good argument and one which resonates with me.

I have recently read of a Gallup poll conducted with several thousand workers in the UK asking about people's perceptions of work. The results were quite astounding. Only 14% of the respondents said that work fully satisfied and engaged them as individuals. 62% said they merely tolerated their jobs, with 24% stating they actively despised their work. That is an absolutely crazy situation.

Elfed and I agree that meaningful work is crucial in life. This is something that our church should have an active interest in. I suggest to him that perhaps the church should consider setting up new social enterprises in different areas to provide work and services to the community. After all, we're not short of a bob or two, with something close to thirty million pounds tucked away in investments and buildings, with more money coming in regularly with churches closing left, right and centre. It would show that the church still has relevance for today and still has a heart for people and their lives.

This issue of finding meaningful and purposeful work for people is also sure to be a huge issue for Ein Gwlad over the next few years.

I'm still wrestling with the faith/politics conundrum. On occasions, I feel perfectly fine about it, even speculating that a new spirituality however that is defined and a political movement for independence could prove to be an unstoppable force in modern Wales.

On other days I'm not too sure. I'm a bit worried about the communications role. It's all well and good working in the background, but what if I'm expected to be more visible and more voluble? How would people in the church respond to that I wonder? And I still haven't mentioned this politics thing to the rest of the members on the course, even though I'm particularly friendly with both Tim and Elfed.

I ponder all this lying in bed at Trefeca that night. The peace and tranquillity is palpable, punctuated only by the occasional hoot of a stray owl.

Howel Harris, the founder of Trefeca wouldn't be happy at all with such political involvement, I think to myself. But then, he was Mr Unconventional himself, what with him combining his role as a preacher and organiser with regular stints in France as part of the local militia. And let's not even start on the complexity of his relationship with his 'muse,' Madam Bevan, which scandalised the faith community of the time. Maybe I can sleep easily tonight after all.

June 25th 2018

I come back from Trefeca to find that another mini-crisis seems to have engulfed the Steering Committee. We had provisionally booked the Diplomat Hotel in Llanelli for the launch in August, although the event itself was yet to be officially confirmed.

For some reason Big Gee had taken leave of his usual careful mode of operating by providing James with a list of all our registered supporters (around two hundred names). James has then taken it upon himself to send out a letter to all these supporters, inviting them to the launch, with the letter adorned with his own signature. I think he's seen Gwilym's personal signature on some of the letters and he's thought he'd like a piece of that. All hell breaks loose when word gets out.

James, to be fair to him, was only being his usual enthusiastic, if slightly impulsive self. I'm sure he gets frustrated having to work alongside grumpy middle-aged men. But, he doesn't help himself when he tries to say that he thought that this had been sanctioned, seeing that Gwilym had sent the list of registered supporters to him by e-mail.

He then tries to blame the general lack of ordered communication within Ein Gwlad structures for the faux pas. Maybe he has a point. After all, I'm not the most organised and effective person on the steering committee by a long way. And I'm supposed to be the Communications Officer!

But Gwilym is having none of it. He sends a strongly worded message to James, like a slightly exasperated headteacher telling off a promising but wayward pupil:

'James, there are clearly defined guidelines when it comes to official communication. That's why we have a Communication sub-committee and a Communications Officer to prevent cock-ups like this! Blaming other people is not the solution.'

Royston then pitches in complaining about the social media blur that we all have to negotiate on a daily basis, which is enough to drive anyone to distraction (let alone a 19-year-old university student preparing for his end of year exams):

'I struggle to keep up with all the information sent to me via: a) comments on my blog, b) direct messages on my blog, c) comments on Facebook, d) messages on Facebook, e) emails, f) Twitter, g) texts, and also various people shuffling up to me whispering " Hey, guess what...?"'

It is a good point. We seem to be drowning in a sea of random information in life in this day and age. Ein Gwlad is no different with e-mails and messages being fired off by all of us on our general Thunderbird e-mail platform. It's all very exciting and absorbing - but there is a real danger that we are becoming unfocused and haphazard in our proceedings.

Gwilym then proceeds to set-up a specific thread on the forum for the Steering Group members, with a directive that all discussions be staged on that thread, with the Thunderbird platform to be reserved for any general news and messages.

Everyone seems to be back on message. For the time being anyway.

There's one funny social media contribution that comes to light after Mike Murphy posts about the creation of Ein Gwlad on a website called 'VoteUK Forum.' A guy called Richard Allen posts:

'Hopefully, this party will at least provide a bit more entertainment than Plaid Cymru, who are without a doubt the most dull, tedious, humourless, miserable and downright pointless party in the UK.'

Humour should definitely be on EG's agenda, I think. People are just fed up with pompous and po-faced politicians preaching down at them, pretending to know the answers to everything. Maybe they will respond better to a party which shows some humour and lightness in all that they do.

June 29th 2018

The tortuous Brexit negotiations drag on. It is becoming clearer by the day, that PM Theresa May plans to keep us as closely aligned to the EU as possible despite the result of the referendum in 2016. In a few weeks' time, the Minister supposedly leading on the Brexit process, David Davis resigns from the Cabinet, followed closely by Boris Johnson.

It appears that Davis has been side-lined by May for months, with another Brexit unit, led by her Civil Service chief, Olly Robins, doing all the real negotiations. Davis has been stitched up completely. As has everyone else who believed that the government would act in good faith in negotiating the UK's exit from the EU, after the largest democratic vote ever recorded in these isles.

It has been an incredibly underhand and devious move by May. What she lacks in any gravitas and leadership ability she seems to make up for with her low cunning.

One of my friends from my journalism days of old, Huw Prys Jones has taken it upon himself to be the main 'remoaner' in the Welsh language media. Huw pens a number of articles claiming that the Leave vote was down to racists and those with a hatred of outsiders, with the 'Leave' voters mis-led and misinformed by unscrupulous Leave campaigners.

He also says that it's a form of virulent English nationalism which is sure to endanger Wales's very existence as a nation. He urges politicians in Wales to work together to fight for another referendum to overturn the original vote. I admire

Huw's passion for the matter and his tenacity in presenting his arguments. But I have to agree to disagree with him on this one.

Huw obviously has a point that a resurgent English nationalism could be lethal for Wales. But I think that a growth in nationhood in England can only be good for Wales. Huw believes the English will never content themselves with 'Just being Merely English'. Even if they agreed to that, there's no doubt it will be a huge challenge for them to build a coherent sense of nationhood bearing in mind the huge divide that exists between London/South East and the rest of the country.

But history shows us that even the most fractious and divergent nations can merge together when they have to, and there's no reason why England can't develop into a modern and democratic country either given the opportunity after Brexit. And good and friendly neighbours to Wales as well.

Stephen Morris, who has a first-hand knowledge of the English mind, living as he does over the border in Shrewsbury, posts on this issue on our forum.

'I don't see English nationalism as necessarily being adverse to our cause. I think your average Englishman these days feels sufficiently beleaguered that he doesn't feel the need to dominate his neighbours to show off what a man he is. I certainly think that Plaid Cymru's constant 'remoaning' will make the party look even more irrelevant once we are out of the EU and if Ein Gwlad can paint a strong, positive picture of an Independent Wales outside the EU, but having good relations with our neighbour in these isles, we will be well placed to garner support.'

I still maintain that Brexit is a revolutionary act, which will completely upend the old model of governance here in the UK. I think the past two years have brought three crucial elements to public awareness:

The sheer incompetence and hopelessness of the Westminster government in handling the Brexit process so cack-handedly. The old public deference towards Westminster's authority is fast disappearing.

It has exposed a growing divide between the political class at Westminster and ordinary people on these isles. The gap was there before, but Brexit has turned this into a Grand Canyon.

It has also shown that it is England, and England alone in the driving seat in Theresa May's 'precious, precious union'. Wales and Scotland are not even sitting in the back seat, they are consigned to the boot.

Nothing can surely be the same ever again after the emergence of those three post-Brexit realities.

Plaid Cymru used to have a slogan 'Independence in Europe.' Perhaps Ein Gwlad should change this to 'Independence in Britain.' I dream of a situation where England, Scotland and Wales are three sovereign nations on these isles, who can then choose to work with each other if need be.

There is a perfect model for this already in existence in Scandinavia. There, Norway, Denmark and Sweden share a land mass, but are three distinct nations who sometime choose to co-operate with each other. The Scandinavian model with their strong individual national identities, market economies and compassionate social structures seem a great example to emulate.

The idea of 'Independence in Britain' would perhaps lessen the traditional fears about independence meaning a drawing up of the drawbridges and isolation which has always plagued the Welsh national cause.

People in Wales have close ties with England and Scotland in terms of family links, and shared experiences by means of popular culture etc. These are much more meaningful ties for most people here than any ties to Europe, important though Europe is in the wider picture.

And the notion of Britain has an emotional resonance here as well. After all, Brythoneg – the precursor to Welsh - was once spoken all over Britain. From Caeredin (Edinburgh) in Scotland to Onnau Meigion (just outside Birmingham) to Rhydychen (Oxford) in south-east England, these place names are clear signs of that inheritance.

Even the Welsh name for England (Lloegr) actually means Y Tiroedd Coll - The Lost Lands - which show how constant a theme that has been in the Welsh narrative along the centuries, after the Welsh retreated to the Wales of today in the wake of the tide of Anglo-Saxons who swept into Britain after the departure of the Romans in the 4th century.

A famous Welsh poem, Armes Prydain, composed in the tenth century urged two rulers, Cynan in the north and Cadwaladr in the south to join together to repel the Anglo-Saxon tide, and the poem concludes with a confident declaration that a Welsh ruler over Prydain will once again be on the throne and the Welsh tongue restored throughout the land.

An Independence party should be bold and fearless in staking the case for Welsh Independence. But it should also be generous towards England and the English. After all, England was once our land and who can ever hate his own land?! Hell, we'll even allow them to re-discover the depth and beauty of their own long-lost language! That really would be a win-win situation for all concerned.

June 28th 2018

Gwyn comes up with a brilliant idea for the launch. He makes the point that Neil McEvoy's launch of his 'Propel' group within Plaid earlier in the month received little or no media attention, despite it being well organised and well attended by all accounts. So then, let's do it without the media!

The idea dawns upon him following his experiences with Cymru a'r Byd (an organization which fosters links between Wales and the World), when they were hoping to organize a choral concert to raise money for the organization. With all the problems involved in actually arranging a venue etc., they finally settled upon just recording the choir performing and then placing that performance on the web for all to see. It worked perfectly well.

Why don't we do the same asks Gwyn? He says we can employ a professional media company to film the launch for us, then we can release the video of the event on the net to all our registered supporters and other interested parties.

The idea fits in perfectly with the kind of different and original thinking image we want to project with the new party, and all the steering committee members sign up to Gwyn's plan.

It is also a firm statement concerning the approach we have agreed to take concerning the media. Everyone is singing from the same hymn sheet in saying that the new party needs to challenge and call out media bias and manipulation from the outset and take no prisoners.

All of us have witnessed the way the media have managed to bully and coerce all politicians and political parties in Wales and the UK for the past generation or so. There's a feeling as well that the general public are now fed-up with the media's sense of its own self-importance and power in setting the agenda for everything.

The case of the veteran singer Sir Cliff Richard, and his success in a libel case against the BBC in the High Court a few weeks later seems to confirm all this yet further. The singer wins a considerable amount of damages after the BBC decided to film a Police raid on his home following a single historical abuse complaint against him, live on prime-time TV. He was not arrested, and no charges were ever laid against him, but yet the BBC decided to be judge, jury and executioner against him - just to flaunt their status and power and improve their ratings.

In awarding damages to the singer for reputational damage, the judge was scathing about the BBC in his verdict. What's interesting is to see the huge amount of public support for Cliff Richard after all the trauma of his trial by media and the legal trial itself, and how little support there is for the usual 'freedom of the press' arguments trotted out by the media.'

I can't help feeling it's bit of a turning point in how the media are perceived by the public and public confidence in challenging the media's dominance in our society.

Gwyn agrees to get in touch with two or three media production companies to ask for prices. The consensus is that we shouldn't cut corners here so that a broadcast-quality video in both Welsh and English will be filmed and distributed to all our supporters and other interested parties. The media can pick up on the story later if they want - but we won't be beholden to their inbuilt biases by doing it this way. The tail won't be allowed to wag this particular dog!

It is also decided that the launch will seek to be as inter-active as possible with the registered supporters who turn up. With around two hundred of such supporters, we estimate that around 25% of those supporters will turn up (50). The room at the Samuel Centre in Llanelli only holds sixty anyway so even if less than that number makes it down to Llanelli on the day, we won't all be rattling round in a huge empty space. It's agreed that we ask the production company to conduct two interviews with Ein Gwlad officers.

It's later decided that Gwyn Wigley Evans and Stephen Morris will be the ones to step up to the plate. Stephen will be doing the English language interview and Gwyn will be doing the Welsh language interview. The Communications Officer will content himself with a low-key background role on the day. Well, Gwyn did say that I could do my work in the shadows. I'm only taking him up on his word!

PEN PORTRAIT 8

Dennis Morris.
Born in Abergwaun. Living in Newport (Pembs)

My name is Dennis Morris and I was born and bred in Pembrokeshire. The Welsh language was not taught in my school (Haverfordwest) in the **60's** but I remember being fascinated and envious of some of my friends, from the North of the county, who were fluent in our mother tongue.

After school I joined the army and spent most of the time away from home with very few visits. During my military service the draw towards Welsh nationalism grew stronger, this was mainly due my experiences in service and the books I read on Welsh history. Regrettably, like our language, Welsh history was not taught at school.

Having lost a few years in the wilderness, after my military service, I became a Close Protection Officer (bodyguard). I spent the first few years with various celebrities before taking up a five-year post in Afghanistan. My clients worked on humanitarian projects that were financed by various governments.

So here I am, after two pointless spells with Plaid Cymru (plus other movements that have sprung up over the years) I've joined Ein Gwlad. I feel these are exciting times, finally we've a serious Welsh nationalist party in the making, a party whose primary objective is to gain full sovereign status for our long-suffering nation.

July 4ᵗʰ 2018

After weeks of speculation about a Plaid Cymru leadership election, the deadline date sees two candidates throwing their names into the ring. Ynys Mon AM Rhun ap Iorwerth and Dinefwr AM Adam Price will both challenge the existing leader Leanne Wood. It seems odd that the two have left it so late to announce their candidature. The present leader has had several weeks to prepare for this eventuality, and this factor seems to give her a crucial edge at the start.

A few days before he throws his name into the ring, Adam Price bizarrely floats the idea of a co-leadership ticket between himself and Leanne Wood - only for this to be refuted by the leader. Adam Price has long been tagged the 'mab darogan' (the promised one) over so many years, doing nothing at all to damp down such extravagant talk - and it seems odd that he would want to share any leadership. But then, Adam has form on this type of thing.

Adam is undoubtedly a thinker and inspirational speaker. But, he sometimes gives the impression of being akin to a kangaroo on speed, jumping from one idea to the next without really developing any of his ideas fully. It makes me tired just to think of all the different ideas he's touted over the past few years- from ARFOR - A Welsh-speaking local authority for the west - to TREFENTER (a brand-new Welsh-speaking town in the West) and GLANNAU MENAI (a similar enterprise on the banks of the Menai Straits) and now this failed co-leadership idea.

Earlier in the summer, Adam had published an article in a London Sunday newspaper, calling for an income tax increase of one pence in the Welsh pound to improve education in Wales. But then during the leadership race, he publishes another article calling for Welsh taxes to be slashed to put 'more money in Welsh pockets'. Inconsistency seems to be his only consistency.

He gives the impression of being an individual who gets easily bored and is constantly thinking up new initiatives to stave off his terminal boredom. But, to be fair to him, it must be very easy to get bored with proceedings at the National Assembly. You only have to watch the proceedings on its own TV station sometimes - Senedd TV , to get bored out of your own mind very quickly.

The nature of the chamber itself doesn't help. It looks like a local council on stilts. It just doesn't seem to have any sense of presence and grandeur worthy of being the nation's prime forum.

Most of the Assembly members seem to spend most of their time gazing listlessly at their computer screens, rather than listening or even engaging with the members who are speaking on any one debate. What on earth is so interesting on those computer screens?

As it happens, gazing at computer screens would turn out to be a particular problem for one senior Plaid AM a few weeks down the line, and create a huge crisis of confidence for Plaid Cymru in turn.

The second challenger to throw his name into the ring the very same day is Rhun ap Iorwerth, the AM for Ynys Mon. He's ex-BBC and thus viewed with some suspicions by many within the party for being a Johnny-come-lately. But he has undeniable presence. Tall and striking, and supremely self-confident. I'm sure he doesn't have to read any inspirational quotes about how to become an Alpha Male.

Rhun's main problem would seem to be the nuclear elephant parked right on his doorstep. As a party, Plaid Cymru have long been opposed to nuclear power, with its members consistently upholding that policy in its annual conferences.

But the party leaders have somehow managed to change this opposition to an opposition to 'new stations on the Welsh mainland'. This of course, is to accommodate the fact that a new nuclear power station is being developed on the island - Rhun ap Iorwerth's seat.

It's a ridiculous contortion of language. This is the kind of thing which gives politicians a bad name. And which makes members and members of the public cynical and suspicious. The nuclear issue was to be a big problem for his campaign from the very start.

There was another nuclear issue to attract a good deal of attention during the leadership campaign - the application by the owners of the Hinckley Point nuclear reactor to dump 320,000 tons of waste and mud from that site near Cardiff Bay. This was fast becoming a real cause of public anger and concern. Why was this nuclear rubbish being dumped on Wales - without even a full Environmental Impact Assessment undertaken? It seemed to be typical of the sheer contempt and disregard that Westminster had for Wales. A month previously, Westminster had rejected a tidal energy scheme for Swansea Bay, which could have been a world first in that particular technology. That had seemed a slap in the face. The Hinckley Point waste seemed a full-frontal assault.

The suspended Plaid AM, Neil McEvoy leads an impassioned public campaign on the issue which eventually leads to an almost unprecedented Plaid/Conservative motion at the National Assembly to suspend the dredging firm's licence to dump the waste material, pending more independent testing of the material. Their attempt however is foiled by Welsh Labour, by 26 votes to 22. There are however 60 members at the Assembly. Where were the other 12 members for such an important vote?

All this was most unfortunate for Rhun ap Iorwerth since it once again alerted people to the long-term problems and dangers involved with nuclear power and as such, his support for Wylfa B seemed even less credible than it was before the contest even began. His two opponents in the race (with some even speculating that they were working together) were to use this stick constantly and effectively against him.

The two even managed to convey the idea that their joint anti-nuclear ticket was a brave and courageous policy on their behalf, when such a policy had actually been in place for twenty years at least. It really was brazen hypocrisy. But then, they are politicians, what do you expect?

Oh, hold on. We want to be politicians as well! Well, some of us do. Can I just stick to writing about them please?

Neil McEvoy, frozen out of the leadership race and seemingly isolated within the party, comes up with a good line, describing the Bay designated to take the waste as 'Geiger Bay'. The area was traditionally called Tiger Bay. Neil McEvoy was one of the speakers at a well-attended anti-nuclear rally outside the National Assembly, the day before the Ein Gwlad launch.

The Leader, Leanne Wood appears to have a big advantage as the incumbent in the leadership race. Usually, in these scenarios, an existing leader has stepped down and a party can engage in an exercise which is all to do with the future, free from the past. This time though the past, present and future will be mixed together.

Plaid members are notoriously loyal. You could even term them as masochistic in one way in view of all the disappointments and let-downs they have endured at the hands of their party over the years. I wonder if they have it in them to knife an existing leader? I tend to think that Leanne's line, "Just give me three more year to finish the job," might be the strongest line of all the lines to be communicated during the course of the campaign.

I have a lot of time for Leanne Wood on a personal level. I will never forget the fact that she took time out from her busy election campaign in the Rhondda for the 2016 Assembly elections, to send me a hand-written note to wish me well when I was ill. I didn't really know her all that well, but maybe she knew that I had supported her bid to become Plaid Leader back in 2012. That little gesture meant a lot to me at the time.

This ability to reach out to people on a one-to-one basis was likely to be the basis of her leadership campaign. She might not have the soaring rhetoric and debating skills of her challengers, but she seems warmer and more human than both Rhun and Adam, who both seem quite detached and other-worldly at times.

An early poll amongst the membership seems to confirm my earlier assumptions. Leanne Wood is supported by 39% of the members, Rhun ap Iorwerth by 15% and Adam Price by 13%.

It's a conundrum for Ein Gwlad. The general feeling amongst the Steering Committee to begin with was that no contest was the best outcome. Royston speaks for many of us in saying that Leanne Wood remaining in place would be a great recruiting sergeant for Ein Gwlad.

Gwyn agrees with this analysis saying he knows of up to a dozen figures in the party who will abandon ship if Leanne is re-elected. Gwyn says we have do our best to help Leanne, win this election whatever way we can. It's a funny kind of support I suppose.

Gwilym takes a different view, arguing that electing Rhun ap Iorwerth as leader would be off-putting to many people in the south who would then be more open to Ein Gwlad.

However it pans out, it's obvious that Plaid are now going to be at loggerheads with each other for some months. It seems to me that this contest has being building up for some time and a lot of personal scores are waiting to be settled.

Over the past year or so, Plaid have been dogged with division and dissension in the ranks. Leanne Wood has managed to lose the services of both Lord Elis Thomas, who has now declared himself to be an Independent, and Neil McEvoy who has been suspended in the space of less than two years.

She will lose a third member of her group in very dark circumstances later on in the month.

And it's not just problems in the Bay either. It seems this malaise is to be seen in all parts of the party.

A month or so previously, no fewer than forty branch members at Llanelli were thrown out of the party over a long-running rift over selection of candidates for election. Apparently, Leanne Wood had appointed a personal friend of hers, Mari Arthur to fight the 2017 parliamentary election over the choice of the local party. Those members had been very vocal in their criticism of this move.

Some of the excluded members included individuals who had been members for thirty years and more. It just looked like a party coming apart at the seams, day by day. With the members of both the Labour and Conservative parties at war with each other after Brexit, it seemed that Plaid had decided to join this endless circle of in-fighting and recrimination as well. It seems that once parties get a taste for this kind of internal attrition, it then becomes a meme which infects the whole organisation.

Later in the month, the level of vitriol in the current campaign becomes clear to all. Nigel Copner, The Party's National Treasurer resigns, citing 'threats' made by the leadership, after his branch in Blaenau Gwent decides to endorse Rhun ap Iorwerth. This is shocking news.

Nigel Copner had arrived from nowhere to come within a few hundred votes of defeating Cabinet Member Alun Davies in the Blaenau Gwent Assembly election in 2016. Surely, such an individual should have been treasured and feted by the party - not threatened and brow-beaten.

Apparently, Nigel Copner was informed by the party leadership that his branch could forget any hopes of support to develop in future, after snubbing Leanne Wood in such an open fashion. The Leadership immediately issue a statement saying they 'have no recollection of such an exchange'. They sound like weasel words. They sound like something that Labour leader Jeremy Corbyn would say.

In fact he did say something quite similar a few weeks later when an old story surfaces of Corbyn laying a wreath to commemorate the Palestinian terrorists responsible for the Munich massacre of 1974."I have no recollection of laying a wreath," he says. Corbyn has always struck me as being a very evasive individual, but this took that personal trait to new levels somehow. It's not a good look for Leanne or the contest itself to be honest. It's a taste of what's to come.

Writer and Plaid sympathizer Jasmine Donahue sums up the febrile mood of the contest, and how social media in particular is being used by the respective camps to attack and denigrate their rivals in an article published on nation. cymru during the contest.

> 'The vituperation, slander and smear of this campaign taints everyone who is engaging in it - it is damaging to the party and to the prospects of securing the trust of those wavering voters they need' she writes.

It's obvious that Leanne and her supporters are well dug-in for the battle ahead. They will use all the tactics at their disposal to ensure that their woman wins. With also a built-in advantage on the NEC-Plaid's ruling committee, Leanne will be hard to beat. She's also got the 'progressive' and 'feminist' cards to play, which are not only a well-proven winning ticket within Plaid structures but are also seen to be automatically virtuous qualities in today's society. Those cards can be played at any occasion.

I think back to the hapless meeting called by Neil McEvoy at Y Celt in Caernarfon a few weeks earlier. The translator for the evening actually pitched in himself during the meeting. Strictly speaking, translators are not supposed to take part themselves in meetings. We are supposed to be neutral observers after all. But then, I'm a good one to say that thinking back to my own experience of flouting that rule at the first meeting in Aberystwyth.

According to the translator in question, in one NEC meeting, Leanne Wood had suggested that Plaid Cymru should call for a bank holiday for the Monday when Wales were taking on England at the Euros in 2016. The translator, Gwynfor Owen, claimed that he had said that this was a ridiculous proposal, only to be promptly sent out of the room for 'abusing' Leanne.

This was a time when Momentum were running rampage within the Labour party, settling old scores with the Blairites who had ruled the roost for so long ,and instigating widespread deselection processes against Labour MP's not deemed to be sufficiently 'on message'. Corbyn seemed to have lost all control of events. An anti-Semitism crisis was going from bad to worse, with the party for some reason failing to sign up to an internationally recognised definition of anti-Semitism. The Ex-Chief Rabbi actually calls Jeremy Corbyn, 'the most offensive public politician since Enoch Powell'.An opinion poll in September shows that 30 per of voters thought Corbyn was anti-semitic.

Labour were looking like a disorganised rabble increasingly in thrall to the hard left.

But the unpleasant incident with Nigel Copner showed that the Authoritarian Left was alive and well in Wales as well.

July 11th 2018

The World Cup has been on for a couple of weeks, and I've been watching avidly as per usual. It's been a great World Cup - one of the best I can remember. I've watched every single one in fact since that 1970 tournament in Mexico where I was completely beguiled by the brilliance of the Brazil team and hooked on the beautiful game ever since. The names still trip off the tongue almost 50 years later. Pele, Tostao, Gerson, Rivelinhio, Jairzinio, Clodoaldo, Carlos Alberto. Best team ever? It's not even a question.

This time round, all the dire predictions about Russian hooliganism and Russian inefficiency have been dispelled completely. A colleague of mine suggests quite seriously that Putin must have built a couple of gulags to house all those hooligans who created such havoc among English fans two years ago at the Euros in France.

Mike Murphy, who has been working in Siberia, assures me that Putin did not have to do this. Apparently, he just sent out the word that he expected all the hooligans to respect Russia's big moment on the world stage and uphold Russian national identity.

"All the people just love him in Siberia, warts and all," says Mike. *"Despite all his dodgy bank accounts,"* he adds with his trademark wit.

England for once have been doing well in the competition, and they eventually manage to get through to the semi-finals where they meet Croatia. They've even won a penalty shoot-out against Columbia for heaven's sake. That's unheard of. The media are crowing that 'football is coming home' – a soccer song composed to reference the fact that England once won the World Cup back in 1966.

The semi-final is a real David and Goliath tie, a nation of 60 million against a nation of 4.5 million. The media as usual think it's a complete formality for England. They're talking about the final already. Luka Modric, Croatia's inspirational midfield player is to say after the game that the English media's dismissal of Croatia's chances was a prime motivator for his side.

I love Croatia's anthem. I'd put it up there right with Hen Wlad Fy Nhadau as one of the very best national anthems around. It's called 'Our beautiful homeland'. It's almost a love letter to a land in effect, calling Croatia beloved and wishing the land to be blessed forever. It then goes on to pay homage to Croatia's landscape - its plains, its mountain, its rivers. It's just an inspirational call to arms. In fact, I think it is even better than Hen Wlad Fy Nhadau.

All Welsh people can relate to this passionate love for our landscape - it's a much under-appreciated element of the Welsh national cause I think. This love and attachment to our land, the very ground of our existence must surely become part of Ein Gwlad's message.

The Croatian anthem is then followed by that awful dirge of an anthem praising a monarch and urging that monarch to continue to rule over them. It somehow sums up everything that's wrong with England today. The Croatian players are singing about their homeland. The English players are singing about a queen. Who do you think has the psychological advantage there? Doh! Croatia win 2-1.

There's a hilarious spat on ITV after the game between two of the pundits. Former Ireland player and manager, the tetchy Roy Keane, can't hide his delight that England has lost after all the hype that they were going to cruise to the final.

"Yous wos planning da final already- yous wos planning da final already - before dealing properly with Croatia!!!" he crows at the distraught Ian Wright.

"And yews a grown man as well," he adds bizarrely, glaring at Wright. It's a brilliant, unscripted TV moment.

Most Welsh soccer fans would have loved all this. This doing England down often appears to be small-minded and chauvinistic to people living in England. "Why do you want England to lose," they ask, with a sense of bewilderment and hurt. "We would always support Wales and Scotland if they were playing countries like Croatia," they say. "Why can't you support us in the same way?" It seems a fair enough point at first glance.

I actually saw this, "Please, please support us," dynamic in action in a pub in Dolgellau on my way back from an SC meeting that month. This lad, from the north of England, part of a touring group of visitors, was actually pleading with a couple of local Welsh lads in the pub to tell him that yes, they would support England in the rest of the competition. He seemed desperate for their support for some reason.

The two of them managed to humour him very successfully, without actually signing up to anything of the sort.

The long and tortured history between Wales and England is obviously a factor in all this. But, it's never been about the English people as such. It's all about the media.

For as long as any Welsh person can remember, blanket coverage about England soccer matches has been beamed into our homes and pubs with this royal 'we' as the dominant theme- that we are all England and all supporting England, although the BBC and ITV are also broadcasting to two different national audiences in Wales and in Scotland at the same time.

There have never been any sensitivities shown to the fact that these particular audiences might have a different take on it all. When you've had that constantly for two generations, it does tend to stick in the craw to say the least. But it's all to do with the media's unthinking bias over many, many years and people here's natural reaction to that. It's not about people, it's about power. And the mis-use of that power by the main propaganda outlets of the British State.

Even though Croatia are later defeated in the final by an ultimately fresher and stronger French side, it's an incredible achievement for such a small nation to reach the final.

As Slavan Bilic, the Croatian ex-player and manager puts it on live TV, with Welsh soccer manager Ryan Giggs standing beside him: *"This is great for all the small nations in the world; for nations like Wales,"* he says gesturing at Giggs. Amen!

July 18th 2018

After several attempts, a meeting is finally arranged between Ein Gwlad and Yes Cymru to see if there is common ground that could be explored between the two organisations. The initial arrangement is that two members of both organisations will meet up on a Saturday morning in a café in Dolgellau.

Gwyn and I are chosen to represent the Steering Committee, with Iestyn ap Robert and Rhydian Hughes as Chair and Vice-Chair representing Yes Cymru. Iestyn then informs us that he won't be able to make it as he has another Yes Cymru meeting lined up at Aberystwyth the same day. Fair enough.

But our suggestion that he find a replacement from the YC Central Committee falls on deaf ears. It turns out that only Rhydian Hughes will be coming along. It's the first sign that Iestyn ap Robert is not all that keen to play ball with Ein Gwlad. That particular feature is to become even clearer as the weeks roll by.

We are having a sustained period of good weather this July. It just seems so unusual somehow. It brings back memories of the scorching summer of 1976 of my teens and those seven weeks of carefree teenage freedom.

I enjoy the journey down to Dolgellau. Wales looks even greener than ever, despite all the heat. I never tire of looking at the amazing scenery all around as I travel down in the car. There's always some new feature of the landscape to notice and marvel at during the journey.

'In Wales there are jewels to gather but with the eye only. A hill lights up suddenly; A field trembles with colour and goes out'.

As usual, the famous Welsh poet R.S Thomas completely nails it. Being rich in a conventional sense may not be a feature of life for that many people here, but as the great man goes on to say,you can indeed 'grow rich with looking,'in Wales.

We have a very useful conversation with Rhydian at Dolgellau. He tells us that there has been some sort of putsch within the YES Cymru central committee, and four members asked to leave. Apparently, this is related to the rumours that had been circulating previously about a hard-left faction within YES Cymru, who were trying to hitch the organisation to that particular vehicle.

Rhydian tells us that he had been given the name the 'Enforcer' and a brief to sort out this problem which was threatening to scupper all the progress YES Cymru had achieved over the past few months. Rhydian has an imposing physical presence, so you can see why the name was chosen.
The ex-Boxer with the Preacher-Communist grandfather had now apparently achieved his aim.

"Yes Cymru is now in a much better place," he declares. *"We are back as the broad church we are meant to be."*

We agree that it would be good to have a mutual 'non-aggression' pact as two organisations - that we don't necessarily have to support each other, but we won't seek to damage each other either. Rhydian tells us that Yes Cymru have around 1,000 members, thirty different groups around Wales ,and around 10,000 people following them on Twitter. It's quite an achievement in eighteen months.

Gwyn suggests that it makes sense for the two organisations to work together since we have the same end in mind. I don't mention the idea of YES GWLAD this time round - it's better for that to develop organically.

But I do suggest that there could be some form of wide political platform for independence in place by the National Assembly Elections of 2021 which could feature Ein Gwlad, Yes

Cymru, Plaid Cymru and other associated groups. Rhydian seems quite amenable to that idea. It's impossible not to like Rhydian. He comes over as a passionate and genuine individual.

Despite his success in enforcing the recent purges within Yes Cymru, or maybe because of those purges, Rhydian is not sure whether he will be re-elected as Vice-Chair later on this summer. He might then rejoin the Ein Gwlad Steering Committee he ventures.

It's a good constructive meeting, and I post up a short summary of the discussion on the forum that night.

It all goes go tits-up within a day or so. Royston puts a short article up on his 'Jac o The North' blog mentioning the fact that four members of YES Cymru have had to leave the central committee. He later tells us that this information has been relayed to him by members of Yes Cymru itself, and it's nothing to do with the post on the forum.

But, it's not just the information relayed objectively. Royston seems to take great relish in the fact that the four lefties have been ejected from the YES Cymru committee. One senses that he's had to take a good deal of stick from the left over the years, and he can't hide his delight at this humiliation for the 'brovvers'. He's really stuck the knife in and twisted it.

Rhydian texts me to let me know that all contact between Yes Cymru and Ein Gwlad is now to cease following Royston's article. The implication is clear, Rhydian is being blamed by Yes Cymru and Rhydian is blaming us for letting the cat out of the bag about this following the meeting in Dolgellau.

Apparently, Iestyn ap Roberts the Chair of Yes Cymru has sent a letter to all members on the central committee to say that no co-operation will now occur with the 'gossip mongers ' of Ein Gwlad.

Gwilym and Gwyn get in touch with Royston, and he agrees to take the offending article off his site.

It's a generous gesture, but you feel the damage has already been done.

There's even more fall-out. Royston then decides to resign from the Steering Group following the incident meaning that we now have no treasurer, a month or so before the launch. He sends out a message to all the members of the Steering Committee saying that it was better for him and for Ein Gwlad for him to resign.

He argues that the blog and his membership of the steering committee represent a clear conflict of interest. He thinks that it's more important to continue his blog than remaining a member of the SC.

The rest of the group accept his resignation sadly. It's a huge blow to lose someone of Royston's many years of experience, his political intelligence, and his commitment to the cause. And on top of that he's a great bloke as well. Tidy, as they would say back in his home city.

But there's a general feeling that Royston has done the right thing here. People were constantly referring to Ein Gwlad as Jac's party. That could prove to be a real millstone around our necks.

Big Gee then composes a letter to Iestyn ap Robert, seeking to calm the waters between us. He explains that the relevant information had in fact been revealed to Royston by members of the Yes Cymru group themselves, so there was no fault to be attached to either Rhydian or Gwyn and myself.

He reiterates the common ground that exists between us and asks for a formal meeting between three officers from each organisation to see how we can co-operate in future. It's a very conciliatory and well-reasoned letter.

But there's no response from Iestyn ap Robert.

A text from Rhydian suggests we could be waiting quite a while. Yes Cymru seem to be wanting to keep their distance from all political parties at this stage. In one sense, you can't blame them. After all, they've managed to attract a 1,000 members in a fairly short period of time - by being beyond all political parties, so why change a winning strategy?

But, this sense of ideological purity was to become problematical for Yes Cymru later that year as they attempted to transform themselves into a limited company. This seemingly innocuous move led to rumblings of discontent amongst the foot-soldiers. This was about a 'power grab' by the central committee based in Cardiff with plans to alter the Constitution to slash the governing body's numbers from 16 to 8 and scrap their national Committee entirely This is made up of members from the various Yes Cymru groups around Wales.

Two members of the original governing body quit in protest. four members of YES Aberystwyth are then suspended for having the temerity to question the changes, and a member of Yes Caernarfon is also suspended temporarily, so that an internal investigation could be held into an apparent attempt by that group to derail the re-structuring process. This without actually being told what the specific charge was against him. This was beyond bizarre. There was feverish talk that the real reason for the changes was to allow for the possibility for Yes Cymru to reconstitute itself as a political party in its own right. Our old friend Neil McEvoy was apparently at hand to step in once that was set up.

YES Aberystwyth write a no-holds barred letter to the central committee expressing their deep concerns about the situation and the very future of the organisation. The letter mentions meetings being arranged with a day's notice and members not able to attend, then being suspended willy nilly, resulting in a situation where only five members of the original sixteen strong committee are now still in place.

They demand that the new Constitution be withdrawn, that all members who have been dismissed be reinstated and an invitation to return to the ranks extended to all members who have left over the past year.

The suspended Yes Caernarfon member, Iwan Rhys, also posts a strongly-worded article on nation.cymru outlining members' concerns about the proposed constitution and appealing to members from all parts of Wales to travel down to the annual general meeting to be held at Porth Tywyn on October 13 to vote against the changes. When that meeting eventually takes place, a compromise is hammered out with the main proposed constitutional changes dropped for the time being and an Emergency General Meeting called in three months time.

Externally, things were looking so promising for Yes Cymru, with the increasing interest in the idea of Independence. Internally though, it seemed as if regular bouts of fratricide were becoming par for the course within the movement,and threatening its very existence.

What is it about today that makes it almost a badge of honour in the current political arena to inflate minor disagreements beyond all proportion and for everything to be so febrile all the time? It's like everyone's taking a new drug, with a trade name of 'let's all fall-out together'. It seems to be addling everybody's brains right now. The Conservative Party, The Labour Party, UKIP, Plaid Cymru and now Yes Cymru as well. It almost seems rude on our part not to join in somehow......

Gwilym waits in vain all summer for a reply from Iestyn ap Robert. But to be fair, Iestyn has got his hands full right now purging all his internal dissidents. He doesn't want to take on a combative Cardi as well now does he?

July 25th 2018

Another political bombshell hits Wales. And Plaid Cymru in particular. Their AM for Mid-Wales and West, Simon Thomas from Aberystwyth has resigned suddenly. His website and twitter account have been cancelled overnight.

It soon becomes clear that this more than your usual run of the mill resignation. Dyfed-Powys soon confirm that Simon Thomas has been charged with the use of offensive images. That's code for stuff involving kids. This is truly shocking. He's been bailed to appear in court in a month's time. The Police later ask for another twenty-eight days to quiz him, and a court hearing against him for 'creating offensive images of children' is eventually set for October. At that eventual hearing, the former Plaid politician pleads guilty to a charge of creating almost offensive 600 images involving children. Images classified as being in the worst possible category.

Can politicians' stock fall any lower in Wales? It's the second hammer blow to Plaid within a few days of each other, following the resignation of their National Treasurer, Nigel Copner. The party just seems jinxed. Personal and family misfortunes aside, this seems like another boost for Ein Gwlad.

It's obvious that the party have had advance warning of this Police investigation and within a fairly short space of time, the second member on their list for Mid and West Wales, Helen Mary Jones is parachuted in to the Assembly in Simon Thomas's place. That seems like another gift to be honest.

Helen Mary is a very high profile and experienced individual: but she comes over like just another moralizing, high-handed politician obsessed with progressive 'ishoos'. I don't think the public are in the mood for another politician of that nature, especially in view of what became of her predecessor in the role. And maybe she's not all that popular amongst her fellow members either.

Big D, who follows Twitter closely alerts me to a post from someone who congratulates Helen Mary for her 'sacrifice' in giving up her post at Swansea University to become an AM. Who pops up next to respond? Her fellow Plaid AM Bethan Jenkins.

"What sacrifice?" she asks. I have a feeling this contest is going to be very entertaining. Who's getting the popcorn in?

July 28th 2018

Royston's decision to resign from the steering committee has left a big gap obviously. But he's not resting on his laurels at all. Oh no. Over a period of weeks he pens a series of brilliant blog posts entitled 'Weep for Wales' in his Jac o the North blog. The posts display his usual searing polemic, allied to a huge amount of research and digging for evidence. One of the recurrent themes of his blogs over the past few years is the corruption, feather-nesting and crony relationships built up between Welsh Labour and the Third Sector. The Third Sector has grown at a huge rate in Wales at present, but they remain a law unto themselves, since they don't seem to be accountable to anyone.

Jac has always maintained that the relationship between Welsh Labour and the Third Sector is based on naked political opportunism. Labour don't get many votes in rural areas in Wales, so their political influence in those areas is very small or even non-existent. But, they have very conveniently found another way to exercise some control in these area just the same - by awarding huge sums of money to some very questionable projects, and the ensuring that their placemen/women are in prime position within these organizations. Another common theme is the ridiculous amount of public money handed out by the Labour government to different projects and enterprises in Wales.

It is just one expose after the other from Jac. But, none of these ever seem to be followed up by those people who are supposed to be the Media in Wales - the Western Mail, BBC and ITV. It seems that Jac's writing is just too raw and close to the nerve for them

In the 'Weep for Wales' blog posts, he exposes a huge scam carried out by a couple of business partners, Paul and Suzanne Williams. These two seem to go from place to place, buying places up, but then letting them go to rack to ruin. Eventually, we find out what the scam is. They are selling these businesses for huge prices to themselves and being able to raise a huge amount of money by means of mortgages arranged by a friendly accountant - who has actually spent time in prison for fraud. It could well be a front for money laundering as well.

It's a staggering piece of research from Jac and his blogs attract a huge new readership. Which is useful for Ein Gwlad as he has an EG banner with joining details on his blog as well.

Files of evidence and testimony presented to him by individuals who have suffered under the Williamses, are now passed on to North Wales Police.

Within a few weeks Jac has more than justified his decision to resign from the EG steering committee and focus on his investigative work with the blog. Heaven help us if Jac ever decides to turn his beady eye upon Ein Gwlad. There'll be no room for sentiment that's for sure despite the fact that he actually got the ball rolling for us. We will all have to behave ourselves...

July 30th 2018
American President Donald Trump arrives in Britain for a three-day visit. There are protests arranged in several cities throughout the UK, with the media hyping up all these protests to almost a hysterical level. It seems that a serious illness called

Trump Derangement Syndrome has struck thousands of people simultaneously. What exactly are the objectives of all these protestors? What do they hope to achieve?

A huge inflatable baby Trump replete in a nappy with a dummy in his mouth is actually flown above London. Some people have clubbed together to pay some £20,000 for this. The Mayor of London, Sadiq Khan has allowed this to go ahead, ridiculous a gesture as it is.

There seems to be some serious confusion in the ranks of the Trump protestors. On the one hand people are accusing Trump of being a ruthless megalomaniac who is oppressing millions of people in America and then he's portrayed by the very same people as a helpless baby in a nappy with no power or agency whatsoever. It just doesn't compute at all.

I've no time for Trump. I don't like boorish and ego-driven people like him. The scandals about him keep turning up such as hush monies paid out to several ladies, who are - how can we best describe them? - active in the adult entertainment field. They have apparently entertained the president himself. Fairly regularly it would seem. There's fevered talk of impeachment. America seems to be going stir crazy.

Trump's got a hide like a rhinoceros. There's no apology or contrition from him. He just says in a matter of fact way that yes, he paid them money, out of his own pocket not from campaign funds. It's like he's re-writing all the rules concerning how public figures should act when scandal hits.

I guess he's also banking on the fact that a lot of Americans will consider these women as just gold diggers.

But, I've got to admit I find his press conferences to be hilarious. Trump loves to bait and wind up the Liberal media, who then work themselves up to even greater levels of frenzy against him. Which in turn just bolsters his support amongst his base. Beyond that folksy, almost simplistic language of his, I suspect there's a very clever and shrewd mind at work.

There were a couple of Trump moments which made me laugh out loud again.

There was one media interview with one anti-Trump protestor on the streets of London. The interviewer asked him why he was there. "I don't like Trump's policies," was the reply. The interviewer then asked which Trump policies, in particular, he was opposed to? After some thought, the interviewee then said he couldn't think of a specific policy he was opposed to.

"I'm just here for the party I guess," he then admitted sheepishly.

There was also that excruciating moment when Trump and May held the press conference in the garden at Blenheim Palace. You could see that Trump could sense blood in the water, and that Theresa May was a dead woman walking.

He was asked a question whether Boris Johnson would make a good Prime Minister. Usual diplomatic niceties would dictate that he deflects such a question, and lavish praise on the present PM. But not Trump. Oh no.

"I think Boris Johnson would make an excellent Prime Minister," he said with Theresa May glaring up at him by his side.

Could he then expand on that, came the reporter's question? As usual Trump brought it back to himself. His favourite subject in the whole world.

"Well, he's said some very nice things about me," he says, in that deadpan style of his. I actually laughed out loud and spluttered my tea on a newspaper on my lap when I heard that.

It's an on-going political pantomime in the UK at present, and Trump's performing the role of the wicked dame perfectly.

PEN PORTRAIT 9

Lee Michael Felton:
Born in Port Talbot. Living in Cydweli.

My name is Lee Michael Felton, I was born the 1st of December **1979** in Glynneath, a typical Welsh Valleys village at the top end of the Neath Valley on the border with Rhondda Cynnon Taf. It was a small knit community where everyone knew everyone else and a lot of curtain twitchers and gossipers.

I moved away from Glynneath in **1999** to live with my, now wife, in her hometown of Port Talbot **1999**. We lived in there for twelve years then moved to Kidwelly, where we have been for three months. We were married in **2012**, we have five children, two boys and three girls.

Reasons for Joining Ein Gwlad

I grew up in a Labour household. My mam was and still is a staunch Labour party supporter and member. My dad was a miner in Tower colliery in Hirwaun during the **80's** and always voted and supported the Labour party. It was my mother that got me 'into' politics and it was her that attempted to bring me into the Labour fold during my teenage years. The **80's** were turbulent to say the least; the family being directly affected by the Miners strikes against Thatcher's dismantling of the working classes way of life. Even as a youngster I felt it was wrong. It's a feeling that has stayed with me through to my adult life. My mother's attempt to bring me into the Labour party was soured by the fact that I didn't like how Labour lacked ambition for Wales. They always seemed happy to accept whatever was given from Westminster, even if what was offered was shit!

I began to resist the push toward Labour and looked elsewhere, towards Plaid Cymru. From about sixteen/seventeen years old up to the my 30's I always voted Labour, even though I felt more 'Plaid Cymru'. The line of 'wasted vote' rang in my ears every time I made my mark at the ballot box so continued to vote Labour.

I finally broke the cycle at the Welsh Assembly elections, I forget what year it was, but I voted Plaid Cymru for the first time. I voted for what I wanted. I wanted independence for Wales. Even from that young age I felt independence was better than what Wales was getting. I turned 35 and decided I'd become a member of Plaid Cymru and actually do something instead of moaning about it, so I got involved.

But, after a few years it was slowly dawning on me that Plaid Cymru didn't seem that interested in independence, they wanted power before anything else. There was also an underlying creeping in of bullying and suppression of criticism within Plaid. I first saw evidence of this in Llanelli just after May 2017 council elections. It was a year later I left Plaid and it wasn't long after that I heard rumours of a new party, that party was Ein Gwlad. So, here I am.

August 1st 2018

The whole nation seems to be going crazy for cycling. It's the Tour de France, and this year the Welsh cyclist Geraint Thomas from Cardiff is going great guns. The media in Wales is going into complete overdrive about this success, especially the Welsh language media (Radio Cymru and S4C – who are broadcasting the race live).

It's a great scoop for S4C who have been struggling of late to appear relevant and interesting. It's an undoubted sporting success for Wales but the hyperbole and the over-dramatization of the whole process is way over the top for my liking.

Sport has been elevated to unprecedented heights in modern Welsh life. Sport, and sports coverage is one of the strongest holds the media have on the public by now. With so much of news being covered elsewhere with the growth of social media, individual blogging and the emergence of citizen journalism - sport is now perhaps even more important to the media's sense of itself, its sense of self-importance and its inherent need to be setting the agenda for everyone.

It's amazing how this seeps into public awareness and how we, everyone, seems to have to partake in the media's narrative.

Having said all that, Geraint Thomas seems a great bloke. He's very Welsh in so much that he comes across as grounded, humble and unassuming. It's amazing to think that he is the 3rd World class sporting star to emerge from Whitchurch High School in Cardiff, following in the footsteps of his contemporaries, Gareth Bale and Sam Warburton.

You could argue that those two stars also display the same characteristics as Geraint Thomas. They must be putting something in the water in Whitchurch.

Geraint Thomas is now actually going to win the Tour de France. Maybe it's not such hyperbole after all. I watch the last stage of the proceedings at my friend Charles's house in Llannefydd, in the Vale of Clwyd. Despite my initial scepticism about the whole process, it's an amazing sight to see G holding the Welsh dragon aloft on the winner's podium in Paris, with the iconic Arc de Triomphe in the background. You can't imagine any better free publicity for Wales on a world-wide stage.

The only bum note struck is the singing of the British national anthem, God Save the Queen after Thomas is formally declared the winner. There's a sardonic little smile on G's face as if to say: "Do we really have to listen to this absolute dirge of a song? And by the way, you know it's not my anthem, right??"!

A week later, Geraint Thomas is feted by a several thousand strong crowd outside the Senedd building as part of the

National Eisteddfod held this year for free in the Bay. The crowd strike up his signature tune, 'Titw Thomas, Titw Thomas, Titw Thomas Las - Geraint Thomas, Geraint Thomas'.

Bizarrely, a minor ditty written by the folksy Welsh-language trio Hogia'r Wyddfa back in the 60ies, and forgotten by all and sundry for many years, has now been adopted as Thomas's signature tune and sung by thousands of his followers.

It seems a seminal moment somehow. Too often, the National Eisteddfod exists in its own bubble, full of its own self-importance, not really having that much impact on the wider public consciousness in Wales. In seeing Thomas outside Y Senedd in front of a sea of adoring fans, you felt that the Eisteddfod, for once, was tapping into the Welsh public mood .

Departing First Minister Carwyn Jones's frank admission that Geraint Thomas had achieved more for Wales in three weeks than he had achieved in ten years was a further nod to the public mood. Honesty from a Labour politician in Wales at last. Things are definitely changing here!

August 4th 2018

The Steering Committee meet up again at Y Morlan in Aberystwyth. Gwilym, Gwyn, James and I are joined by Mike Murphy this time. He is back home in Wales for a while from Siberia. Mike is working as civil engineer in Siberia at the moment.

Big Gee is getting a bit wound up. With only a few weeks to go before the official launch, the registration process with the Electoral Commission has hit a stumbling block. Royston had been dealing with the issue, and he has agreed to see it though although he has now resigned from the SC.

The intention to take over Ioan Richard's registration of his 'People's Representation Party' has hit the buffers because there's some difficulties getting the paperwork from Ioan and there's no guarantee that these will be processed by the Electoral Commission by the time of the launch.

Gwilym lets off some steam about a lack of adequate preparation and whether everything will be in order by the end of the month. It now appears that the process of taking over the registration of a previously registered party is much more time-consuming than anyone had originally anticipated.

We decide that a new application has to be submitted - this can be done over the internet. Although we have not yet chosen a leader or deputy leader, the Electoral Commission insist on having two official names on the application. Apparently, these can be changed at a later date. I propose Gwyn as leader and he readily accepts. Mike Murphy also agrees that his name be placed on the registration.

A few days later, the Electoral Commission come back to say that they need a third name on the application, and Stephen Morris, holidaying in Northern Ireland eventually agrees to become that third named person. Everything seems back on track. But Gwilym's concerns about getting all our ducks in a row are to reach new heights a couple of weeks later when we understand that the idea of just taking over the original bank account set up by Royston Jones in Ein Gwlad is a non-runner.

As it's a savings account it's a 'no-can-do' from the Bank. Without a bank account there'll be no opportunity to persuade the registered supporters to become full members at the launch and following the launch. It's not looking good, but who comes to the rescue again is Gwyn, Ein Gwlad's Mr Fixer. He manages to set up a bank account for Ein Gwlad with Santander.

But the Electoral Commission keep on creating new hurdles to be cleared right up to the launch itself and even after the launch itself, eventually declaring that they cannot accept Ein Gwlad as a name on a new political party. This is due to the fact that Gruff Meredydd's old Sovereign Wales Party, also has an additional reference to 'ein gwlad'. Fortunately, Gruff is willing to bail us out, agreeing to drop this part of his own party's description so that the Electoral Commission's objections about potential clashes between names and confusion for the voters can be overcome.

At the steering group meeting Gwilym also complains about the lack of volunteers coming forward, despite a couple of appeals which have been made on the supporters' forum. Two key roles remain unfilled, the Party Treasurer and Party Secretary.

I try and cheer him up by suggesting that perhaps the supporters are just waiting from some more meat on the bone, and more specific details about Ein Gwlad before they will consider getting really involved. And maybe they are still wading through the meaty newsletter that was sent out to them recently. Big Gee doesn't look convinced, I must say.

On reflection, that newsletter was too long with too much detail included. Even so, it did lay down a clear marker as to the kind of party Ein Gwlad was hoping to become. A fully participative political party with a clear mission to move away from the top-down structures of the established parties of Wales and the UK.

'It has been proposed that we set up a national policy forum where individuals from the wider public (whether they are registered EG supporters or not can make suggestions and air their views.) This is something that other syncretic parties in Europe have experimented with - especially in Denmark- with striking success. This is due to the fact that instead of having discussions behind closed doors by politicians who think they know what the public want, the public themselves are invited to present policies on issues that concern them - after all, shouldn't all parties work in this way. At the end of the day, they are supposed to be the servants of the people not their masters.

Ein Gwlad feels strongly that it should be led by the public in its policy-making processes as our aim is to make Cymru a better and more prosperous country, and its citizens should enjoy more freedom within a free, sovereign state. The freedom of the individual is important to us. People should not be weighed down by petty rules, ridiculous bureaucracies and constant surveillance. Neither should they be governed by a nanny state. Free people in a free country is our aim.

The various forums set up by Gwilym and the two parked websites in both Welsh and English which would go live after the launch are a good launchpad for the type of digital and participative democracy we want to develop.

But as important as those forums are for facilitating this type of development, it also has to be tied-in with a renewed emphasis on face-to-face politics, where people are involved, engaged and inspired to seek change in their lives.

There's some new evidence that social activism and dedicating yourself to a cause beyond yourself and rooted in the wider society where you live can be good for people's emotional and mental health. A book by Johan Harri called 'Lost Connections' has just been published where the author claims that the mental health epidemic across the western world is caused by a break-down in society. It's not a case of broken brains at all he says, but rather broken societies.

I think he's right. All too often nowadays we have people opening up about their mental health issues, and everybody cheers and says that opening up and being honest will cure everything. That's undoubtedly helpful but it's too individualistic. People won't get better until our society gets better. We need a renewed society where people talk to each other, engage with each other, work with each other, and share and dream together.

I'm always envious when I hear my parents talk about their experiences of growing up in different parts of rural Wales in the 1940s with the strong extended families and community ties all around them. I know it's easy to romanticize the past, and it wasn't perfect by all means, but when my father talks of his childhood growing up in Pontiets, Carmarthenshire where he and his brothers knew the names of everybody in that village, and which managed to sustain a thriving social and cultural life themselves - I think something very important has been lost.

I love hearing my dad chat with his two brothers when they meet up. Having lived up in the north for so many years, he's lost the distinctive Carmarthenshire accent of his brothers, but when they chat together, he sometimes slips back into those lilting western tones, and time seems to stand still.

I might be biased because of my family links there but think that Carmarthenshire is the most beautiful county in the whole of Wales. I'm glad we are launching in Llanelli.

A few days later, some good news arrives via the forum. A Phillipa Roberts, a chartered accountant from Llanrwst has volunteered her services for the role of Treasurer. A woman! At long last! Let's hope we don't all fall over each other in welcoming her to the next meeting. Steady on now lads...

A couple of days later, we also have another recruit. Lee Felton from Cydweli - who was formerly quite heavily involved with Plaid in the Llanelli area - has agreed to give Das a helping hand with the social media side of things since he is quite experienced in that area. Lee is a freelance graphic designer and his skills and understanding of how best to use social media quickly become apparent to us all.

A couple of weeks later, there's another recruit to the Steering Committee - Sian Caiach from Llanelli, a doughty campaigner and whistle-blower about public life in Carmarthenshire. She has been part of a local group called Gwerin Gyntaf/People First in the county campaigning for more transparency and accountability within local authorities. She'll be a fantastic addition to our ranks.

Things are looking up. I told you not to be so glum about things Gwilym!

August 9th 2018

An interesting thread is developing on the supporters' forum. Although no specific policies have yet been drawn up, with Mike Murphy charged with co-ordinating this process, one idea that is attracting a lot of discussion is the idea of a Citizen's Income.

This would at a stroke, replace the whole current benefits system, and award a set sum to each adult citizen to be spent as they see fit. The point is made that this could be a radical, flagship policy which would engender a huge amount of interest and potential support

I'm instinctively suspicious about a Citizen's Income. I have always felt that a newly independent Wales will need all hands to the pumps to make it a success - we need people to become entrepreneurial, dynamic and ambitious for themselves, their families and their nation. Isn't there a danger that a Citizen's Income where people would probably work less would work against all those factors?

And how easy would it be to really reform a benefits system which is so deeply ingrained in Welsh society and to which people are so emotionally attached? There must be also be a possibility that people would only abuse a Citizen's Income system.

But Big Gee frames it in a sense of learning to trust people once again, after having been conditioned by Westminster to be automatically suspicious and distrusting of people for so many years.

"We need to get away from preconceived suspicions about people. Most people are sensible, decent and principled, they need a bit of freedom to demonstrate that. Instead, we have a lack of trust and crippling negative suspicions regarding our citizens," he says.

Meirion Wyllt does the calculations and works out that an annual sum of £15,000 for every adult in Wales would amount to £37.5 million - just over the entire Welsh annual budget.

But other posters point out that this figure would most likely be much less in view of:

The savings incurred with the loss of 90% of staff 'managing' the current benefits system

Less fraud investigations concerning benefit claims

Less court costs

Less prison costs

Along with an increase tax take with people starting up more new businesses in Wales.

The argument develops in a new direction with LMF (Lee Felton) arguing that a Citizen's Income should not be a stand-alone policy and that it should be part of a complete package of changes.

"If we do 'x' to benefits, we are also going to do 'x' to education and 'x' to employment as well," he argues.

Eos Pengwern agrees that it should be a complete package: with Citizens' Income aligned with a flat rate tax system as well as some scaling back of state expenditure. He's also very enthusiastic about the system:

"In my view, selling the advantages of a citizen's income and its advantages is a key part of selling the advantages of independence itself," he claims.

Merion Wyllt expresses some concerns that if people quit their existing jobs with a Citizen's Income along with public workers laid off with the end of a benefits system, a gap will appear which might have to be filled by a further influx of people from over the border. Others suggest that some sort of a residency qualification of 3 or 5 years would have to be put in place to avoid that kind of scenario.

Penddu pitches in with a good point about disabilities. Would those with disability conditions be covered by a Citizen's Income or would this need to be an additional facility he asks? The consensus seems to be that discretionary disability payments would still need to be in place as a safety net.

Big Gee sums it up well.

"At the end of the day, we won't get the votes from those who do not care all that much for independence, our language and culture etc, but if we show them that their personal lives could be transformed with something totally radical that no other party has touched upon - and personal motivation kicks in - it is a sad fact that the vast majority out there don't care much about anything - apart from their personal well-being and that of their family"

It's a really interesting debate and shows the forum at its best yet again, a collaborative effort with robust and creative thinking encouraged. I'm starting to be a bit more open minded about a Citizen's Income.

It has the potential to be a truly transformative idea. With a set income in place for each adult in society, this could allow people to find meaning and purpose from a wide range of activities in life from starting businesses and enterprises, engaging as citizens, and building new social networks here.

I wonder if a Citizens' Income could also be linked to some form of commitment to lifelong learning where people are encouraged to update their learning regularly, with learning defined in the widest possible sense.

We need to fall in love with learning again as a nation. And learning together at all ages.

After all, learning together has been a clear historical theme in Welsh history. When the Laws of Hywel Dda (Good Hywel) were codified in the 10th Century, (becoming the most advanced Legal Code in Europe at the time) these weren't imposed from above. Rather, Hywel Dda sought out wisdom from all parts of Wales in drawing up his laws. It really was an early Learning Together example.

This learning together theme was also seen in the early 18th century, with Griffith Jones's circulating schools which brought people together to learn to read in their own communities. This project managed to make Wales the most literate nation in Europe at the time.

And the first universities in Wales which were set up in the 19th Century weren't established by royal decree or patronage as in other places. Rather they were financed by the people of Wales themselves who went into their meagre pockets to be part of a national crusade to provide education and new opportunities for their children.

A new emphasis on education and learning allied to a Citizens Income could inspire the Welsh people again.

August 8th 2018

I travel down to the National Eisteddfod in Cardiff and manage to arrive at the Chapter Theatre by 6.00 pm to watch the Director's Cut of a film called 'The Ballymurphy Precedent'. A mate of mine, Gwion Owain has been involved with this film as a producer, dealing with the financial side of the production. I sit beside Gwion at the back of the theatre.

The 'Ballymurphy Precedent' tells the tale of the shooting of eleven innocent civilians in Belfast at the hands of the British Army's Parachute Regiment, a few months prior to the Bloody Sunday shootings in Derry. In many ways, Ballymurphy was a practice run for the events in Derry - but the story has not received a fraction of the attention given to the latter. I myself had not heard about it until Gwion's involvement.

The film merges original footage from the time, with a reconstruction of the shootings and personal testimonies from the families of those individuals killed. It also includes two very honest interviews with two former soldiers who served in Belfast at the time. They not only admit that the British Army messed up big time, but that these events actually triggered all the resulting violence in the province for the next thirty years. This is dynamic stuff.

It's an absorbing film and it really grabs your attention from the off. But about three quarters of the way through, Gwion Owain pokes me in the ribs and asks if I am ok. Apparently, I'm snoring loudly at the back. I know I've had a long journey down from the north but that is no excuse.

I sit up sharply. I've got the producer sitting by my side, for heaven's sake! Gwion watches me closely for the rest of the film in case of any more slacking from me.

There's a very interesting Q and A session with the Director, Callum Macrae at the end who argues that the killings were in fact a metaphor for the way that the British State managed to turn what was a mass civil rights campaign in northern Ireland in the 1960s into a 30-year war. Following years of campaigning from the family for justice, an inquest is to be held into the event later this summer.

The inquest looks sure to lead to the truth being revealed about this event for the very first time. It's likely to lead to yet another breakdown in public trust in the British establishment.

August 10th 2018

It's a very different type of National Eisteddfod this year.

The National Eisteddfod is a nomadic cultural event- one of the highpoints of the Welsh year - with the festival visiting a different part of Wales for a week every August. It features music, poetry, drama, literature, dance, art, popular music, concerts, debates: with all the activities held through the medium of Welsh.

This year, it's being held without an official 'maes' as such with everything located in Cardiff

Bay around Y Senedd and Millenium Centre buildings. It's also for free this year - a big change to the usual set-up where it costs £20 a day to get in. This £20 fee has always been a contentious issue for a lot of people.

Big D always refuses to go the Eisteddfod on a point of principle, since he says the Eisteddfod makes no allowances for someone like himself who is un-employed (although in reality he is employed in looking after his elderly parents near Aberystwyth). But, he's still not going to go this year despite the Eisteddfod being for free.

This time he says that he doesn't want to have to meet the great and the good of Welsh-speaking Wales - who all use the Eisteddfod as a big networking event for themselves and their families. He's got an answer for everything has Big D. But he has got a point.

Once I get there, it soon becomes clear that this Eisteddfod is going to be huge success. It's colourful, informal, and full of people. Many of whom have obviously been attracted there by the fact that it's free.

But a Cardiff blogger named Marcus Stead threatens to rain on the parade with a series of provocative tweets deriding the festival as an 'absolute bore fest' and railing against the 'crachach of Dafydd and Esyllt etc', who he says have a disproportionate influence upon Welsh public life. He points to the fact that 80% of the Welsh population don't speak Welsh.

He also complains about the noise 'on the mice' - which I find to be genuinely funny. The image of people tip toeing around to avoid stepping on the 'mice' all around conjures up all kinds of interesting images in my mind.

Marcus goes on to gripe about the creeping bilingualism of modern Wales, unwittingly revealing one of the key features of bilingualism i.e. how words in two languages in proximity with each other can interact and spark off new creativity and imagination in people's minds. As in 'Maes' and 'Mice' in my case.

The blogger's Twitter account is later bombarded with messages of protest, with some as usual overstepping the mark completely. 'Outrage culture' has reached Wales of course, and the Eisteddfod is no different.

It's quite apt in a way that the Eisteddfod chair, a few days later, is awarded to a poet called Gruffydd Owen, whose work bemoans the growing influence of mediums such as Twitter on people's thinking today. 'Un tsaen hirfaith o'n bitshio anorfod' (One long chain of our predictable bitching) he writes of Twitter.

I find the abuse meted out to Marcus Stead on Twitter quite appalling and totally counterproductive.

There's a very wise and valuable Welsh proverb which goes like this: 'Rhydd I bawb eu barn ac I bob barn ei llafar' (Let people have a freedom to express themselves and let all opinions be aired). It's a proverb which is even more timely and important today in this age of political correctness and speech-monitoring on all quarters.

I think it's very easy when you are in the Eisteddfod bubble to think and believe that everyone thinks the same about things as yourself. There's an irritating sense of smugness and superiority which is unfortunately part and parcel of the Eisteddfod scene.

It's off-putting for a lot of ordinary Welsh speakers like Big D and his ilk. Apparently, less than 10% of the 600,000 Welsh speakers in Wales go to the Eisteddfod. Can the Eisteddfod really be so smug when 90% of Welsh speakers never visit the Eisteddfod?! How are ordinary English-speakers in Wales going to take any interest in it when their equivalent Welsh speakers never do? Marcus Stead is speaking for a lot of these people. He deserves to be listened to.

'There's a Welsh establishment that looks after its own,' he writes. I think he's uncomfortably close to the mark there.

But his cousin, Phil Stead (whom I know vaguely) then writes an open letter in response to his first cousin - who amazingly he has never met - on nation.cymru. Apparently, their great-grandfathers were two brothers who moved to Wales to find work in the coalfields of the south from Hereford in 1901.

It's a beautifully written letter from Phil Stead explaining how he has embraced the Welsh language and culture as an adult, despite it being completely absent from his formative years as a teenager growing up in Cardiff.

He counters his cousin's point about Welsh being something for the 'crachach' alone by referring the vibrant Welsh language world where he works in Caernarfon, where Welsh is the natural, every-day language for the vast majority of the local population, whatever their social background. People will discuss everything, from local events to Love Island and Donald Trump through the medium of Welsh he says. It really is an inspirational piece from Phil Stead, which attracts almost a 100 comments on the site - the biggest response 'nation' had for months.

Marcus Stead then responds to his cousin's letter with a reply of his own. It's a good reply, fair play to him. He refers to the abuse his original tweets engendered, and then argues than rather than branding him as 'anti-Welsh', people should engage in a more nuanced discussion about the role of the Welsh language in Wales today. It's a good point to make. Both Marcus and Phil have made important contributions I think.

Cardiff - for all the progress made by the Welsh language in the capital over the years - boosted no end by the constant influx of Welsh speakers from the north and the west - is still only 11% Welsh-speaking. It is primarily an English-language city and will continue to be so for the foreseeable future.

But there's also a wider point made about Cardiff, and it's influence over Welsh life - both Welsh-speaking and English-speaking. Another poster, who is sympathetic to Marcus Stead's arguments, makes an interesting point about how even the English-speaking Media in Wales, dominated as it is by Cardiff, doesn't really represent English speaking Wales.

He mentions a German friend of his who works in the valleys, but who is bemused to find that the valleys accents are almost completely invisible on the media in Wales. He claims they are 'forgotten people' in reality.

With 40% of the Welsh population living in the Valleys - this is a very important point. This lack of meaningful participation in the media is a metaphor for how these areas are non-participants in other parts of Welsh national life as well. This area will be crucial if the new party is to make any headway at all.

Das (Darren Owen) from Caerphilly is the social media officer for EG. He has some really good insights into the thinking of Valleys folks. Despite the lauding of Leanne Wood, the Plaid Cymru Leader and her leftist credentials in the valleys - Das says that her brand of 'progressive', right-on politics is a turn-off for most people there.

A lot of places in the Welsh valleys have still to be visited if I am to achieve my long-term ambition of visiting every village and town in Wales. I've always found Valleys people to be warm and proud of their communities. They are SO Welsh. With some of the highest concentrations of native-born inhabitants in the whole of Wales.

And although Welsh is not the main language in these communities today, the language is still a persistent influence there. The percentage of Welsh speakers in The Rhondda Valley is only 12%. But as recently as 1901, 72% of the population was Welsh speaking. So, it's still there under the surface. It's great that we have Das on board.

Das is well aware of all the problems that face the Valleys communities, which have never really recovered following the decimation of the mining industry and the loss of thousands of jobs a generation ago. Mining was a tough and dangerous profession, but at least there was a sense of pride and worth associated with those jobs which sustained whole communities for so many years. Nothing has ever come close to it since then. Call-centres and out of town shopping centres don't really compare.

Das points to another feature which has stripped the Valleys of a good deal of its vibrancy over the past years - the closure of many pubs/clubs which used to be the places where working men would come together to discuss politics and society on a face-to-face basis. The introduction of the smoking ban and the increasing offers of cheap alcohol in the supermarkets has meant that many of these important community facilities have been knocked down and turned into flats or gastro-pubs and the like. He says there's now no place for the working man to talk about politics but Facebook- which can be so easily manipulated.

I round off my visit to the Eisteddfod with a few pints on the maes with Gwion Owain and a couple of other friends on the Saturday night. The last day is spoilt by heavy rain and wind, and it's a shame that the Eisteddfod finishes on such a low note, with so few people able to be out and about.

We agree that this year's different sort of Eisteddfod has been a worthwhile experiment, which should be repeated again. One possibility is that a maes-free Eisteddfod of this nature could be held in Caernarfon - the capital of Welsh-speaking Wales - when it visits the north in 2021.

Well it would be, confusingly enough, a maes-free Eisteddfod on the Maes - since that is the name for the popular open-air square in Caernarfon, which has a continental feel to it when the weather is right.

Hopefully, such an Eisteddfod could be held right in the centre of the town, making use of bars, cafes, and other various centres so that the whole town becomes involved and engaged in the enterprise.

This really could be an Eisteddfod which involves ordinary Welsh-speakers in a way that never usually happens. Who knows maybe some of those 90% that never go to the Eisteddfod might be interested this time. We raise a pint to that possibility. Who knows, maybe Phil Stead can persuade his cousin to come up and sample an overwhelmingly Welsh-speaking community where ordinary men and women would not think of speaking anything but Welsh in their everyday lives?

August 11th 2018

The political in-fighting within the Conservative Party reaches new heights, if that is at all possible following months and months of low-level attrition. Boris Johnson, who has recently resigned from the Cabinet following the Prime Minister's Chequers Agreement, is on manoeuvres, hoping to dethrone May by the Autumn.

Johnson is a very unsavoury individual, whose essential nature was revealed for all to see in a memorable TV documentary made by the broadcaster Eddie Mair a few years ago. That documentary showed what a deeply cynical and unprincipled individual Boris Johnson was. But he is undoubtedly a clever and shrewd politician.

He pens an article in the Tories' house paper, The Telegraph. It's purposely designed to rile the party leadership and appeal to the Tory grassroots at the same time. It's concerning the wear chosen by many Muslim women in the UK - the burqa. Although he takes the apparently principled position about not wanting to ban the burqa - he describes burka wearers as being similar to 'post-boxes' and 'bank robbers'. Of course, the real 'bank robbers' - the bankers and traders in the City of London who almost brought the UK to the edge of ruin a few years back and led to a period of deep recession, are let off scot-free by the Bullingdon Boy.

But predictably, Johnson's tactics work. His support rockets. The Conservative leadership walk into the trap set by him. They call for him to apologise. PM Theresa May issues a ridiculous statement saying, "The Burka is not oppressive, and it's a woman's right to wear it". She then announces that an internal party investigation is to be launched and Johnson could be ordered to go on 'diversity training'.

Once again, being the tin-eared politician she is, Theresa May misses the public mood on this entirely. Johnson has played her like a fiddle.

I've no time for Boris Johnson as a person or a politician. And to be honest, this is a bit of a non-issue in Wales itself, with only 1% of the population being Muslim women

But, even so, this issue of free speech is fast becoming a pivotal issue in modern society. It seems that 'taking offence' has now become a national industry with everyone jumping on the bandwagon, claiming to be offended by this and that. There's a 'culture creep' element to this constant monitoring of people's speech that I find deeply disturbing.

At the end of September, a Plaid Cymru councillor called Anne Greagsby from Penarth is suspended for a whole year by a disciplinary committee for using 'transphobic and abusive language'. Her crime? Suggesting that people who have male genitalia and who now wish to self-identify as women should never be regarded as women. Commenting on her suspension, she says that the party seems to be monitoring everything that people are saying nowadays and declaring, "No, no, you can't say that today".

It seems just another example of Plaid being subsumed by a niche issue, taking up valuable time, energy and resources. With 'entrists' using the party as a vehicle for their own particular hobby horses. And the traditional nationalists too disheartened with Plaid's current fortunes to put up too much of a fight to resist their influences.

A blogger called 'Dafis', comments that schisms and diversions have always appeared in national struggles in different countries over the years.

'But, I cannot recall any party in any country being so utterly diverted from their main purpose by people who are effectively third parties, not themselves involved in transition. These are saboteurs, hell bent on using these circumstances in which others find themselves to create a conflict where one does not exist,' he writes.

Gruff Meredith, who appeared at Ein Gwlad's initial meeting at Aberystwyth back in November 2017, writes a brilliant article on this 'taking offence' bandwagon in Y Cymro newspaper over the summer.

He points out that by stopping freedom of opinion as some people seem to want today, this is actually stopping the right of everyone to express their opinions, and leading to a 'groupthink' mentality, where any dissenting views are not tolerated and suppressed. A disaster for a healthy, functioning democracy.

'Give me a free society where it is possible for people to say and think things I don't agree with, or to say stupid things or even cruel things even, any time. The other option is much more frightening,'
he writes.

Surely, in a free society we have to accept that satire, ridicule and criticism at whoever it is aimed has to be at the very heart of society. Christianity has always been the butt of satire and ridicule and has always found ways to live with it.

Why should Islam be any different? You can't but help thinking that this is a case of moral cowardice on the part of the political class who fear the consequences of extending what has been doled out to Christianity for centuries to an equivalent religion. And we all know what those fears are after a number of terrorist attacks in the UK.

The left, as usual have tied themselves up in knots on this one. They say that Johnson's comments are unfair and cruel to a section of society who are already oppressed as it is But why can't they attack the source of that oppression to start with - the patriarchal and misogynist elements which are to be found in Islam?

There's also this incredibly patronising line of thought that these female individuals aren't robust and resilient enough to be able to deal with and brush off such comments, and the left therefore have to leap to their defence! It really is a case of infantilising people.

I tend to think that human beings have evolved to look at each other's faces in the public square. The face is what makes all of us equal participants in the public square. The face is at the heart of who we are, and of who other people are and how we relate to each other in public. This wilful distancing themselves from society and other individuals by a group of people covering their faces - such an essential human feature - does no favours to anybody.

August 18th 2018

It's the morning of the last Steering Committee before the launch. I'm going to try the new T2 free bus service on Saturday between Bangor and Aberystwyth. The bus is due to leave Caernarfon at 7.30, and for one who is notorious for getting to places at the last minute (indeed one church elder has started to refer me jokingly as 'the late Aled Gwyn Job'), I'm in place by 7.15.

I sit down waiting for the bus to arrive, flicking through my newspaper. I look up quickly and what do I see but the Lloyds Coaches Bus - the company running the service - sailing by, with the driver not even glancing over at the seated area where I was sitting, along with two other people. They shrug their shoulders and just slope off.

I'm reminded of the time that Big D and I went walking along Offa's Dyke, and went into a pub at Talgarth in Powys to ask about the times of local buses that day. It was only early afternoon. The landlady just looked at us as if we were slightly slow and said:

"There'll be no buses now today. This is Wales. What do you expect?"!

The other two might have sloped off, but I'm fuming. I won't be at the most important meeting the steering committee have arranged all year. And I'm supposed to be the Communications Officer. Big Gee won't be happy. I've now got two hours to kill before the next bus at 9.30. I text Gwyn to let him know what's happened and to apologise to the committee. No answer from Gwyn. Now's he pissed off as well.

I go to while away the time with my newspaper at a local café. When the 9.30 bus eventually arrives, it's fairly full already but I manage to get a seat. By the time it trundles in to Aberystwyth 3 hours later, it's absolutely jam-packed, a mix of local people taking advantage of a free day out to Aberystwyth and tourists. It's worth seeing the joy on people's faces when they get on and find that it's a free journey.

We've got a clueless Labour government down in Cardiff Bay treating Wales as a region rather than a nation. But praise where praise is due - this free bus service on a Saturday is a great idea and the public have responded positively.

I sit back to enjoy the views, with the immortal words of Conservative Prime Minister, Margaret Thatcher coming to mind: "If you find yourself on a public bus after the age of 26, you can consider yourself a failure in life". Ha, Ha- I don't think Mrs Thatcher realized how hilariously wrong lots of her statements were, delivered with that oh so serious tone of hers.

But maybe the joke is actually on me. The real reason I'm on a public bus today is the fact that I have managed to reach 12 points on my licence, and I have just received a 6-month ban. It's annoying. But, I'm trying to look at it positively. Tesni, fair play to her has offered to chauffeur me around for the next month or so at least.

Emyr, my neighbour, who seems to know everything that is going on locally, informs me that you can buy a weekly Arriva ticket for the whole of north Wales for only £18. I'm spending at least £35 a week on petrol.Hey I can actually save money with this ban of mine... .

My lovely Scottish friend Laura, who works in Caernarfon, tells me of people she knows who have lost their licences for six or twelve months, and who have actually found a sense of freedom by not being dependent on a car. It will be fine.

I'm enjoying the journey. In a car, you are lost in your own thoughts. On a busy bus like this, you feel you are part of an on-going conversation in the form of the chats going on all around you. It's real communal experience.

I'm sitting in front of a Nain (Gran) from Bangor and her teenage grand-daughter from Llanllyfni; the Nain regales the teenager with stories about the family, about uncles, aunts, cousins and extended family - and the teenager is lapping it all up.

It's a sweet, warm and touching conversation between the two of them, and I feel that I'm actually getting to know them just by listening in on their conversation. I later find out there's eight of the extended family on the bus!

It just seems to sum up what being Welsh is all about: family, community and belonging.

I finally arrive at Aber. I grab a quick lunch at Morgan's, but Gwyn phones me to tell me to come over - there's about thirty minutes of the meeting left. I walk in shame-faced, but they're all very welcoming, fair play.

Mike Murphy, Policies Co-ordinator, is just finishing off going through the policy outlines for the launch. A leaflet about these will be handed out to the registered members who come along on the day. To be prepared by Mike, Gwyn and myself on Google Docs. Phew - they still think they can depend on me despite this morning's cock-up.

Stephen Morris points out that an outline of the core policies will be fine since the official policies cannot be drawn up until after the first Annual National Conference later on in the year.

I'm also introduced to our newest member , Philippa Roberts of Nant Bwlch yr Haearn above Betwys-y-Coed - our new treasurer. But then, the meeting comes to an end. I feel a bit frustrated to be honest.

"We've unearthed a real gem here," says Big Gee to me in the foyer afterwards. I tell Phillipa, who confusingly enough wants to be called Phil, that I'm so glad that a youngish looking female has at last joined this group of middle-aged men.

James is a little miffed to be termed middle age, but I'm sure he's aged a lot during all the ups and downs of the past few months. Fair play to James, it hasn't been easy for him surrounded by people who are all a lot older and more experienced than him. I admire him for sticking with us.

Interestingly enough, James tells me he prefers working with older people since he finds people his age so indoctrinated by political correctness, and virtue-signalling and so on. There'll be none of that with us lot, that's for sure.

James has been a constant over the past few months, and I am sure he'll be crucial in any appeal to the younger generation once the party gets going.

We retire to the Rheidol café for a panad, and I tell them about the dozy bus driver who meant that I missed the meeting to all intents and purposes.

Gwyn, typically with all his connections, knows Public Transport expert, Professor Stuart Cole - the guy who actually came up with the free bus idea which has been put into practice by Welsh Labour. He goes out to phone him.

He comes back and tells me that Stuart Cole is fuming about it. That's two of us then. He then provides two emails for me to submit a formal complaint. That's Gwyn to a 'T'. He's such a doer. An achiever. Just the kind of qualities we need to encourage amongst the people of Wales.

The story about the loss of the driving licence which led to the frustrating bus experience gets a sympathetic response. The other new member on the Steering Committee, Dennis Morris from Fishguard, is also having to miss the actual launch on August 28th because he's going to be going on a speeding awareness course that day.

Even the careful and considered Stephen has been caught out twice in quick succession near where he lives in Shrewsbury recently. There's a general consensus amongst us that these traffic fines are a big scam on behalf of GogPlod (North Wales Police). A figure is quoted saying they made a £1 million pounds from these fines over the past year.

"I feel a policy is shaping up here," says Stephen, suggesting that what needs to be done is to place flashing green signals with the speed limit outside every village and town in Wales. He says that people are much more likely to respond to such a visual sign like this than just the normal signs.

Gwilym then says that there are areas in Holland which have done away with speed limits completely - with no increase in accidents whatsoever. He says that people have self-regulated themselves and the new policy has worked. It's a further example of his emphasis on trusting people to make decisions for themselves and to move away from these nanny-state tendencies in modern society.

As usual, I meet up with Big D after the meeting. This time we're going to the Home Café on Pier Street. He's been very impressed with this place after hearing that they opened up on

Christmas Day to provide free food for fifteen local homeless people, as well as other people who were just lonely on the day, which can be very difficult for many people. He's got a real social conscience.

Big D tells me he reckons Adam Price is going to win the Plaid Cymru leadership race.

"He's stolen all your clothes mate," he tells me. *"He's read that Cymro article at the National Eisteddfod, he's been taking the pulse, and he's going to take over your Independence brand and gain all the credit for it!"*

Big D and Adam Price have some history, as they were both members of Young Plaid in Cardiff some years ago. He was also friends with current leader Leanne Wood at that time, so he's certainly had some political education you could say. He says that 'Pricey Boy' as he calls Adam Price, once accused him of being 'all mouth and no trousers'. Big D reckons that's the most prophetic statement that the Carmarthenshire politician has ever expressed in his career thus far.

He's a brilliant mimic, and he launches into his 'Pricey Boy' impression, together with those heavily exaggerated Carmarthenshire tones that Price is so prone to use:

"Well, it's not the BEST time for me personally, but eh, you know if people are calling you Y Mab Darogan all the time, well, you know there's a CERTAIN obligation on someone to respond to that, eh in a POSITIVE fashion."

He's got him to a 'T' and I fall about laughing.

Apparently Big D was called the 'baby-faced assassin' by another contemporary from his Young Plaid days, and another familiar face, the television reporter Ellis Roberts. That's funny in a way because a former girlfriend of mine pointed out the similarity between Ellis Roberts and the Screen Assassin played with such frightening accuracy by the actor Javier Bardem in the film, 'No Country for Old Men'. Now, I can't look at poor

Ellis Roberts on screen without that disturbing image flashing up in my mind.

And I've actually seen his own killer instinct at work in the way he interrogates his interviewees. There was one I remember recently with Bishop Andy John of Bangor Cathedral, who was trying to justify some Church of Wales jaunt with up to a hundred clergy going on some form of church trip to Spain. The Bishop was flailing about, being ruthlessly exposed by Ellis Roberts's forensic and merciless questioning.

I can imagine Ellis Roberts as some sort of Medieval Inquisitor in his black cape, psychologically destroying his victims even before any physical torture is applied.

And to continue with the scary meme, I also think that Adam Price looks quite intense and scary what with those bushy eyebrows of his. He doesn't smile much in any interview I've seen. Let alone crack a joke. Any such examples appear to pain him, as if they ruin his carefully cultivated image of serious endeavour for Wales.

Why do politicians have to be so intense and po-faced all the time? Why can't they be lighter and more humorous? Don't they know that humour is the best way to connect with other people? Welsh people in general are a very fun-loving people. They love to have a laugh. Why are our politicians so deficient in this respect?

I actually met Adam Price some ten years ago on a Plaid Cymru visit to Cuba. I didn't talk much to him because I was probably in too much awe of him at that time.

But, I tell Big D that 'Pricey Boy' managed to get us into a prestigious meeting with the big guns of the Communist Party in Havana. After one or two of their key people had talked to us about how wonderful they were, they then asked if there were any questions. They didn't really look as though they wanted any questions from us to be honest.

But straightaway, an arm went up; Clayton Jones from Pontypridd. A former Hydro member - the former pressure group within Plaid which also featured Gwyn Wigley Evans. I just had a feeling this was going to be uncomfortable for all concerned.

"Have any one of you," he demanded, in his strong Valleys accent, waving his hand along the row of officials on the podium. He waited a few seconds before delivering his punchline, *"Ever stood for election?"*

There was a deathly silence in the room. The officials on the podium stared at Adam Price, on the podium, as if to say: *" Why the hell did you allow the Hydro guy to come here to meet us?"*

Finally, one of the officials composed himself and said stiffly: *"We are selected NOT elected".*

And that was the end of that meeting. Good trip though fair play..

I ask Big D what his latest take is on Ein Gwlad. He has been sceptical from the start and he hasn't really changed his tune despite my involvement. It's good to have this type of 'critical friend' in place with this because I know he will not hold back despite our friendship.

He says he can't see how Ein Gwlad and Welsh Nationalism in itself can change anything in reality: it needs to be part of a wider coalition for change in England. Big D is a big fan of Jeremy Corbyn in this respect. This is a point I have heard before from my landlord Sel at Caernarfon.

It's a fair point I reflect. But then, hasn't that always been the argument in Wales - let's just wait until we can have a transformative Labour government in place at Westminster? It's been a long wait as it is. It's almost eighty years since the last Labour transformative government under Clement Attlee in 1945.

Personally, I've got no faith in the Labour Party. Tony Blair killed the Labour party in my opinion. PM Harold Wilson once declared: "The Labour Party is a moral crusade, or it is nothing." Well, the moral crusade has long come to an end. That just leaves nothing.

The weather's grim and it's rainy and dark on the journey back home. There's a lot less people on the bus on the way back, but there's more Welsh-speakers on the return journey, especially from about half-way onwards.

There's the extended family of eight from Llanllyfni, there's a fewer older women on an outing together, and there's some middle-aged women going out for a Saturday night drink at Porthmadog. And there's a couple of young women, not much older than my own daughter, dressed to kill despite the rain and the cold and planning a big night out in Bangor.

I sit back in my seat, I close my eyes and let the rich sounds of Welsh from these various conversations wash over me. It's a warm, reassuring and heart-lifting experience. I've just been down to the National Eisteddfod in Cardiff where the main prize winners were rightly lauded for their work.

But, for me, it is ordinary people, like these people on the bus, rooted in their own communities, who are the real champions of the Welsh language. Making creative use of Welsh to talk about everything under the sun. With absolutely no material advantages for doing so either.

Clinging to their language and land against all the odds, with pride, tenacity and with… faith. Yes, Faith. That is the right word.

I've changed my mind several times on several issues over the years, but I've always been convinced that any real future for the Welsh language depends entirely on sustaining and developing the language in the naturally Welsh speaking areas in the West. That will also provide support and hope to all the other places in Wales, where perhaps the language is not as strong at present. And it would be a huge incentive for all those new learners who perhaps, would like to be able to practice their new language skills in areas where Welsh is still the community language.

The rain continues to lash down outside, and I run over the figures in my mind for these particular areas once more.

The last census of 2011 showed that Gwynedd was still the strongest Welsh-speaking area with 64% Welsh speakers (down from 60% in 2001); Ynys Mon 58% down from 61%. Ceredigion was down to 48%, and heart-breakingly, Carmarthenshire, the county of my ancestors on my father's side, was down to 44%. For the first time ever, in 1,500 years, our national language is now beneath 50% of speakers in two of the key remaining Welsh-speaking areas.

The Welsh Government has set itself a target of reaching a million Welsh speakers by the year 2050. There're 600,000 Welsh speakers in Wales today. It's a totally arbitrary and meaningless target, pushed far ahead enough to 2050 so no one has to be accountable for the policy.

There's no clear strategy as such in place to achieve this aim. It's just words, just a headline for them. It's just another clear example of Welsh Labour's endless cynicism and opportunism.

It's also a further sign of how the Labour Party have moved away from being a party concerned about the well-being of communities to become obsessed with individual rights and to consider everything from the perspective of individuals and their individual opportunities alone. They just don't get it that language is more than just individuals being able to speak Welsh: it's got to be about sustaining the communities where Welsh is still a living, everyday language.

There's no appreciation of the fact that in what remains of Welsh-speaking Wales, there's a profound sense of hurt and loss concerning the fact that it seems to be that it's not the people leaving the land as much, but the land leaving the people. Welsh Labour don't like to make any connection between the language and the land. It's too politically incorrect and awkward maybe after recent European history. But it's just a cop-out basically.

An author named Carl Schmitt in his book 'Political Theology', talks about a sense of 'existential defeat' faced by peoples today when part of their world becomes less familiar and less resonant, and their connection to it is thus undermined. That seems to ring true in the Wales of today, both Welsh-speaking and English-speaking. Interestingly, this theme of loss, a grieving for place and sense of belonging is also starting to be addressed by a few writers in England as well, in the wake of Brexit. There had seemed to be some form of Faustian pact formed over the past generation or so between the globalists, multi-nationals and the money-people on one hand and the liberal elite's emphasis on the benefits of immigration, 'progressive' issues, and a paternalistic distaste for any form of loyalty to nationhood on the other hand. This had left millions of people bereft and lost and struggling to make sense of things. Mathew Goodwin put it well when he wrote:

'Some assumed that the 'left behind' was only ever about economics, when it was more to do with feelings of social and national loss.'

It really comes to something in Wales, when it has to be UKIP - the party of seven misfits at the National Assembly elected in 2016, and its new leader Gareth Bennett - who ventures to say what all language experts are saying, but none of the other mainstream parties are willing to say: that the majority of the Welsh Government's investment in the Welsh language should be geared towards sustaining and developing the language in its remaining heartlands.

Some people are already suspicious of Gareth Bennett's true intentions here, but there's an old Welsh saying:

'Gan y gwirion ceir y gwir – Sometimes truth comes from the unlikeliest sources'.

August 20ᵗʰ 2018

Nigel Farage, the ex-UKIP leader has announced that he is to make a comeback to frontline politics to challenge the 'Chequers Agreement' currently being touted around the capitals of Europe by Theresa May.

He's a popular hate figure for the Liberal Left of course, which is odd in a way because Nigel Farage is a creature fostered and developed by the Liberal Left when you think about it, in terms of his presence on the BBC's flagship Current Affairs programme, "Question Time". Apparently, he was the most invited politician onto the show between 2008 and 2016. The BBC chasing ratings again, even though Farage's worldview was of course miles apart from theirs.

There's no denying that he's a very good speaker. He's got a way of talking to people as if he's at their level and speaks their language. He's miles ahead of most frontline politicians in that respect. He completely owned the Lib Dems Nick Clegg in a television debate about Brexit before the 2016 Referendum.

And to be honest, I can't see any problem with his trademark call for a new immigration points system for the UK like Australia, where migrants with identified and specific skills needed in the host nation are prioritised. That could in turn make it easier for Wales to introduce a similar policy to ensure that our needs as a nation are also met in this respect after independence. What's good for the goose is good for the gander.

The influx of people from England into Wales has always had cultural drawbacks as far as the Welsh language is concerned, with the language losing a great amount of ground as a result. But there are other more serious repercussions because of the sheer scale of older people now moving to Wales from over the border. For instance, the fact that 30% of Wales's pensioners today were actually born in England. These individuals would have paid their income tax/national insurance in England, but the cost of paying their pensions falls upon the Welsh tax-payers: this now amounts to £3 billion per annum.

Therefore, 5% of the Welsh population who are elderly people from England is actually responsible for an eye-watering 22% of Wales's current deficit of £14b.

The obvious health issues with such an elderly inflow of people is also placing additional burdens on a health service which is already creaking as it is. The Westminster government of course has not offered any form of financial redress for health authorities having to deal with this continuing burden. And of course, not one party in Wales has yet been brave enough to raise this issue, despite the fact that the problems involved are becoming clearer to people by the day I would like to think that Ein Gwlad will be brave enough to confront this elephant in the room.

I have to say that Nigel Farage worries me in terms of the kind of popular appeal he has. His re-appearance on the scene could revitalize UKIP, who have been a disorganised rabble in the National Assembly, and who everybody thought were now on their way out. I fear his newly-found influence and the publicity he will no doubt garner will once again bolster UKIP in an area which Ein Gwlad has identified as a crucial area for the party - the Welsh Valleys.

Over the past few years, UKIP has been actually challenging Labour and beating Plaid into third place in many places in the Valleys. And now, just as it appeared their star was on the wane, who rides into town again but Nigel Farage.

But there's also something more disturbing in his return as well. Politics here is febrile enough as it is. Emotionalism and irrationality are running riot. There's a new 'People's Vote' campaign now being launched by Remainers who now seem to have morphed from being merely 'Remoaners' to being 'Remainiacs'. That's going to be divisive in itself.

And now, the fractious Farage is back. It's like pouring oil on troubled waters. There's the whiff of trouble in the air. All this is not going to turn out well, I fear.

The English poet G K Chesterton once said something along the lines,

"The French rose in wrath first. The Russians followed. We will rise last, and our wrath will be the ugliest".

You can't help feeling that a long over-due reckoning with the political class is all set to take place. One can only hope that Chesterton's dire warning is not enacted.

It's an interesting point to consider that the Farages were originally French Calvinist Huguenots who fled persecution in Catholic France, finding a safe haven in the UK. It is estimated that as many as 40,000 Huguenots came to live in different parts of the UK between around 1680 and 1730, a huge number in view of the fact that the UK's population at the time was only around 5.5 million.

Farage has always sought to establish his European credentials both because of his French Huguenot roots and the fact that he has a German wife. That's been useful for him to distinguish between the continent of Europe and the EU.

Ironically enough, with UKIP usually seen as being Englishness personified, with no regard for Welshness, my ancestors on my father's side in Carmarthenshire were also part of this huge wave of Huguenots into the UK.

As in the case of the majority of the Huguenots, they were also Calvinist Protestants fleeing from Catholic France. The first denoted Job in Carmarthenshire that the family know about was David Job, who was church warden at Cydweli in the early 1700's.

I renew the family connection in Carmarthenshire a few weeks later by staying overnight with my Uncle Hywel at Llansaint, the night before the official party launch at Llanelli. Hywel is a natural comic and he's great company.

Once again, he regales me with hilarious tales about my Dad and their family life when the three brothers were growing up together in Pontiets, a small village outside Llanelli. I love hearing these tales from him. He truly is performing the role of the family historian in all this.

As the stories about the family line continue one after the other, it's almost as if all our descendants who moved to this part of Wales all those years ago are brought to life once again. Carmarthenshire once again becomes a home-from-home for me.

As I travel through the county on my way back up north, I'm just consumed by a sense of love and attachment to this land around me. The land that provided shelter and new hope for some of my forebears. The land that fills my heart with joy, appreciation and wonder every time I travel around it and marvel at its beauty.

It's sometimes difficult to fully explain Welsh nationalism to our English neighbours, whose sense of nationalism and national sentiment is more often than not bound up in symbols of 'Britishness' which exude authority and power. The Royal Family, Westminster, the BBC, Armed Forces and the like.

We don't have those types of symbols of authority to sustain us here in Wales. Welsh nationalism is much more to do with people and their relationships with each other and their communities. And the Welsh language of course which is a core part of the Welsh identity.

But, I think our love for the land even transcends those first two factors. It's as if - in the absence of the clear symbols of power enjoyed by our neighbours in England - the land here has become even more important in the national story. Obviously, we've had to depend on the land for sustenance and support for centuries. But it's always meant even more than that.

Above all possessions, above all material comforts, above everything else in life, we've got the land. And a sense that this land could yet become transformed, once Wales is free.

Back home, I visit Svet and Dale's 'Dome' café in Bangor once again, to do some more writing.

Svet bustles about her café, engaging with every single person there in her own unique, friendly and warm fashion. No wonder 'Dome' has become so popular so quickly amongst local people and tourists alike, although they only started up at the beginning of August.

Svet tops me up regularly with free bottled water to help me along with my writing and I'm getting increasingly hooked on Dale's tasty soup recipes.

As I experience their warm welcome, once again I'm reminded again of the historical importance of being open to different cultures and influences in life.

August 22nd 2018

The launch pamphlets have been printed.

Mike Murphy, our man in Siberia led on this even though he is on the other side of the world. Mike is fast becoming a key player in the new party. Gwyn and I then chip in with our own suggestions. As specific policies cannot be adopted until the first Annual National Conference to be held in a few months-time, this pamphlet is just a holding position in essence. It provides the registered supporters and all others with an outline of Ein Gwlad's main proposals at this stage.

The main heading reads that Ein Gwlad's aim is:

To secure a prosperous and fair Independent Wales

The pamphlet then goes on to say that an Independent Wales would not be worth achieving if the same failed policies of the devolution years are repeated. A radical sea-change is needed with a brand-new political approach.

'Ein Gwlad will be a syncretic party - not left wing, not right wing nor centrist. We will employ ideas from across the political spectrum to come up with practical policies that benefit Wales and her people."

There are six Policy Headings provided on the pamphlet:

Welfare: As Wales is stuck in welfare dependency, the party will develop a Citizen's Income Policy.

Taxation: The party will propose a simpler and more effective tax policy.

Health: The party will seek some private sector investment and new mutual care models in addition to the present public health service.

Economy: The party will foster a new entrepreneurial Welsh spirit to propel the nation forward

Democracy: "The collective wisdom of the Welsh people is better than the selective opinions of a handful of politicians". The party will seek to build a new, fully participatory democracy in Wales

Power: The Party will seek to share power and wealth from Cardiff to other parts of Wales in a fair and equitable manner.

There is also a commitment to sustain and develop Wales's national language and its distinctive culture, traditions and heritage.

It's a great effort from Mike as usual. 'From Russia with Love' you could say.

Even Big D puts aside his usual scepticism about Ein Gwlad when I show him the pamphlet. He thinks it looks impressive. He's particularly taken by the Citizen's Income idea which he feels could be a real vote winner. He says the main points have been conveyed effectively- without giving too much away either.

There are some interesting responses later on Social Media, with the Citizens Income and Tax Policy garnering the most attention. Michael Haggett, who is a leading light with YES Cymru comments that a flat tax rate is not progressive since it would only make higher earners even better off. But, he is more charitable about the Citizens Income idea:

"It would be unfair to expect Ein Gwlad to have worked out all the fine detail on day one. However, in principle, I'm convinced that a Citizen's Income could work. I also suspect it might work better in Wales than in many other countries because we have comparatively few very rich people and therefore less overall variation between rich and poor."

The Western Mail - commonly known as Welsh Labour's in-house newspaper - is shortly to launch a full frontal attack on Ein Gwlad.

Bizarrely, when the paper runs its first story on the arrival of Ein Gwlad, it focuses not on the fact that a new political party has been launched and considering its possible impact upon Welsh life, but rather on the business interests of interim leader Gwyn Wigley Evans(he is a director of a knitwear company based in Macedonia).

Chief Reporter Martin Shipton tries to make out that these goods are imported into Wales, thus undermining Welsh manufacturing. He's wrong as the goods are only imported into Holland and Belgium. There's also a nasty little headline composed above the article including the word 'foreign'.

It's a sign of the dirty tactics that will be used by the established parties to try and silence what they consider to be a bunch of upstarts seeking to upend their cosy little political consensus in Wales.

Once again, a quick-fire collaborative effort on the forum comes up with a clear riposte in the form of a letter to the Editor of the Western Mail. We manage to turn the tables on the Western Mail by developing the business angle highlighted in the article into a positive rather than a negative feature.

"We believe that having two experienced and hard-headed entrepreneurs at the helm of Ein Gwlad will be a huge plus for our party" reads the letter.

"This marks us out as markedly different from the politicos and nothing else, who have dominated Welsh political life for so many years". Although the letter eventually doesn't run after the Western Mail print a fulsome apology for getting their facts wrong, it will surely prove to be a strong and effective line for future use, highlighting the radically new approach of Ein Gwlad.

And Mike Murphy, in his own inimitable way puts out a tweet with the hashtag 'WesternFail':

'Maybe next time they can report the facts and not resort to smears and innuendo'.

August 25th 2018

The launch is a few days away. I'm nervous about it although I've managed to wangle a back-seat role for myself in the event itself. It brings back memories for me.

I've been here before. Back in 2000. I was in a bad place then after a divorce and another totally unexpected change in my personal circumstances. For some reason, I thought that was just the time to start a new party off my own bat. Maybe it was just a diversion from everything that had happened to me in such a short space of time. I don't know.

I was persuaded by an unscrupulous television journalist called Eifion Glyn to record a TV interview about the creation of a possible new party on S4C. He knew full well I wasn't well at the time. He also knew that there were only a couple of other individuals involved and that there was no structure and real planning behind it. He just wanted a juicy story. I was persuaded, against my better judgement, to take part in the interview.

The whole project went absolutely nowhere, of course. For several years after this I was consumed my self-recriminations.

I'm now in a much better place. I've dealt with the past and come to terms with it. It no longer bugs me.

This time it's different. It's not about me. For a start, there's a collection of outstanding individuals involved in the Ein Gwlad project who have all come to the same conclusion that Wales needs a new start.

The media have been kept at arm's length this time to allow plenty of time to think this through. To plan everything properly and ensure that everything is in place before going public. A year of hard work has gone into it. It really has been 'softly, softly, catchee monkey' approach

And then a horrible thought crosses my mind. What if Wales's own Spanish Inquisitor, Ellis Roberts turns up uninvited? And worse, what if he wants an interview? Wales being as it is, it's not impossible that he has heard about it on the grapevine. And he might be aggrieved at not having had an official invite in the first place.

I make a mental note to have a look at the lay-out of Canolfan Samuel, Llanelli which Big Gee sent out to the members a few days previously. The toilets seem a decent step away from the main conference room. That's good to know, just in case I need to beat a hasty retreat...

We have talked a good deal about using humour and lightness to show that we are 'normal' and light years away from the drab, joyless and boring politicians we see all around us in Wales.

I really think that will appeal to the general public. The Welsh in general are a fun-loving people, but this is never reflected in our political life where being worthy and pious about everything is par for the course for the people who appear on our screens.

Mike Murphy's good in this respect and comes up with a great line during this period - in response to Adam Price's call on Plaid Cymru to formally renounce nuclear power and oppose Wylfa B.

This has actually been Plaid's policy for many years, but the politician is now making out that he's creating a brand-new policy for the party.

Mike uses Twitter with the heading: 'We are anti-nuclear. Plaid's new clear Policy.'

Das (Darren Owen) our social media guy also creates a really good meme, drawing attention to the hypocrisy of Plaid's position on nuclear power.

It's great use of humour to make an important point.

PEN PORTRAIT 10:

Sian Caiach
Born in Gelligaer. Living in Llanelli.

My name is Sian Caiach and I was born in the mining village of Pen y Bryn near Gelligaer in **1957**. My father and grandfather were miners there and my mother was a primary school teacher, the first in her family to go to college. My father left the pit to try his hand in the Car Industry and other forms of manufacturing and after a primary education in Wales, I spent my secondary education in England, my father going from job to job meant I attended nine schools in total.

I went to Medical School in London, where I joined Plaid Cymru, qualified in **1981** and came back to Wales in **1983** to work in Cardiff, Swansea, and Church Village before moving to Scotland to study Orthopaedic Surgery in Dundee and Angus. There I joined the SNP. Finally I came back to Wales to take up a consultant job in Llanelli in **1994**. I lost my career in **2005** after exposing a scam whereby local surgeons and anaesthetists ripped off the NHS by using public resources for their private patients. Like most whistle-blowers I was the one victimised after my disclosure, forced to leave my job and blacklisted. The greedy consultants who milked the system didn't even get a reprimand. I was then unable to work in the NHS and other opportunities quickly dried up. It was a difficult time for myself and my children, my partner left me, we struggled financially, but we survived. Depressingly I was recently told that the local NHS is just as corrupt as when I was booted out.

I did become a local councillor in Llanelli but left Plaid in 2009 after it became clear to me that the Plaid County Councillors' group were not willing to support local campaigns which were important to my ward. I was against building on flood plains and wanted to stop the pollution of the estuary with sewage from the overloaded system. Plaid felt building houses to finance the Scarlet's new rugby stadium and clear their debts was more important than the environment. We parted ways. In the end the Scarlets are still in debt and the local environment severely degraded.

I stood for council with the independent group People First/Gwerin Gyntaf and am still a Llanelli Rural councillor.

I have always been a Welsh Nationalist and believe now that Wales desperately needs independence as soon as possible. Since 1999, when their support peaked, Plaid Cymru have been in decline and last year polled only 10.4% of the vote. Independence is not a Plaid Policy, just an aspiration for a later date as our country falls behind the rest of the UK. Our Welsh Labour Government are all for the UK and getting Labour into power in Westminster but show little interest in really improving Wales.

I feel that Ein Gwlad is the best chance we have for a better, fairer and decent country. The old politics, the injustice and the anger in Wales demands action not patience and waiting for a 'right moment' which may never come.

I have a found in Ein Gwlad a young party
filled with good and committed people willing
to truly fight for Wales and achieve a better
future for us and our Children. Ein Gwlad are
not here to help others to get rich or
politicians to get power in London while we and
our neighbours suffer second-rate treat-ment
and declining opportunities. We are not in it
for ourselves but willing to fight as well and
as fiercely as we can for the future Wales
deserves. If Wales is Your Country and you want
to help us, join Ein Gwlad.

August 27th 2018

The Brexit negotiations show every sign of going right down to
the wire. Both the EU and the UK government are engaging in
high risk political brinkmanship to the very end.

Everything is as clear as mud two years after the initial
referendum as far as the UK Government is concerned. No
clarity, no vision, no mission, no purpose, no agreement.
Westminster has really been exposed as never before in all of
this. Things can never be the same ever again after all this
chaos.

With this complete drift on the part of the Conservative
Government, people are being wound up daily by a diet of
media scare stories about no medical supplies, no travel and no
food in the shops if no deal can be agreed in time. The
atmosphere is febrile, fractious, fearful. The words of the
famous Sex Pistols song 'God Save the Queen' and Johnny
Rotten's sneering voice come to mind: "There's no future, no
future in England's dreaming".

The EU and the UK remind me of two heavyweight boxers
slugging it out for fifteen long rounds, going at it hammer and
tongs to the very end. Perhaps both boxers will collapse to the

floor at the final whistle, with both of them broken and no real winner on either side.

But both sides have to come to some kind of resolution by the end of October. So, whatever is agreed can then be presented for consideration by all twenty-seven EU countries, before the arranged leaving date of March 29, 2019.

As for Wales, the narrative here was overwhelmingly a doom and gloom one, with the same apocalyptic scenarios about the implications of Brexit here being painted within the national movement.

"How on earth can you still want Brexit to take place?" people ask me in increasingly strident tones, no doubt influenced by the relentless negativity and scaremongering of the BBC about the whole situation. Yes, it's a risky position to take in one respect - but then isn't life itself risky? And yes of course, such an approach means being in league with some very unsavoury bed-fellows such as Jacob Rees-Mogg, Boris Johnson, Liam Fox and the like for the time being. With their imperial delusions about Britain striding the globe again like some form of modern colossus. However, the other choice was to throw in one's lot with the likes of Tony Blair, Peter Mandelson, Alistair Campbell, Nick Clegg, and the rest of the liberal metropolitan elite, with their demand to 'stop Brexit.' The very people who had ruled the roost for the past generation or so, and who had actually created the clamour for change on these islands by their outrageous feather-nesting and self-serving behaviour over so many years. The people who wanted to maintain the status quo. To keep things as they are for their type of people.

Many people in Wales feared that should the Jacob Rees-Mogg, Liam Fox and Boris Johnsons of this world have their way, the dominance of London and the south-east and even more rapacious type of capitalism would be unleashed like never before here. There's an odd, fatalistic, "these people are always going to win," mentality at work here, even in nationalist circles, the very people who should believe that change is possible.

But, I think people underestimate how one big change can then lead to other big changes in turn. History is full of examples of the vanquished being replaced by the apparent victors, only for those victors also to be swept away by a third wave of response. I hardly think that the north of England and the Midlands will sit back and allow their big opportunity for substantial change to slip through their fingers after Brexit. The voices of these areas will be much more voluble and much more heartened to demand real social and economic change. The old model of UK PLC is bust. It's time is up.

And there are also many influential voices in England also seeing Brexit as an opportunity to completely re-shape the state of things on these islands. To finally jettison the old delusions of Empire and start to build a modern democratic nation in England, where all parts can feel equally valued and validated.

There is bound to be economic disruption and dislocation along the way following Brexit and this will obviously affect Wales. But, I would argue that Wales, being used to life without a lot of money for the most part, and its community-based affiliations, is well placed to deal with any fall-out. It can even lead to a greater sense of resilience here, and a renewed commitment to the national cause. Hard times can be good for the soul of an individual since it can often lead to breakthrough. Hard times can be good for a nation as well.

There was also a wider strategic point to be considered. Brexit, and the way it was being mishandled was fast persuading the people of Scotland that independence was the only escape route. Opinion polls now show support for Independence in Scotland at between 45% and 50%. At the last referendum campaign in 2014, the YES side were starting from a base of 28% support, which eventually managed to reach 45%.

This time any campaign would be starting out with both sides evenly balanced. With Westminster's aura of competence and authority shattered by the events of the past two years, how on earth could they run a credible campaign to keep Scotland tied to Westminster this time round?

But, the situation in Scotland hardly featured at all in the media's coverage of Brexit, even though it really was the elephant in the room.

The SNP who had lost the original Independence Referendum back in 2014 had a mandate to call a second independence referendum, by the end of the Scottish Parliamentary term in 2021.

It was a difficult call for the SNP Leader, Nicola Sturgeon. Some were urging her to wait until after 2021 to be able to fully assess the effects of Brexit. That sounded sensible. But, would the SNP have another mandate to call a referendum at that Parliament, considering they had been in power for ten years by then? It was a big risk to take.

It also seemed as if the ground troops, in the form of the 100 or so YES Scotland groups across the country were getting increasingly tetchy and frustrated with the SNP. They made the very fair point that the referendum had be called before March 29th 2019 otherwise Scotland would be out of the EU. Surely, they had to act before then?

There were also influential voices taking a slightly Machiavellian line on things by arguing that the UK Government did not have the capacity or the energy to fight two battles at the same time effectively. Scotland should strike in the Autumn just as things were coming to a head between the UK and the EU.

A couple of recent polls have indicated that a majority of voters would put achieving Brexit above retaining Scotland, (and Northern Ireland for that matter). UK voters have long been conditioned by the tabloid media to believe that Scotland is a subsidy nation, completely dependent on the goodwill of Westminster.

The truth of course is completely different. Scotland has been more than holding its own for many, many years because of its oil and gas reserves, and its growing food and drink industry amongst other things. Indeed, there's growing evidence that it is Scotland who is subsidising the rest of the UK to all intents and purposes. One of Scotland's premier political websites 'Wings Over Scotland' actually unearthed official state documentation which showed that Scotland had been running a trade surplus ever since 1921! The surplus had apparently been used to sustain 'Imperial Services'. What a grandiose name for wholesale looting of a nation's resources!

The truth is that Westminster are desperate to keep hold of their cash-cow north of the border. But recent opinion polls show the public in England want Brexit more than they want to keep hold of Scotland. How can politicians at Westminster reconcile those two completely contradictory positions?! It's just one huge game of high-stakes political poker. It's fascinating to watch I must say.

The SNP Leader, Nicola Sturgeon is a very canny operator, and some are even wondering whether she has a humdinger of an ace up her sleeve, ready to be played at the right moment. Would she indeed stay clear of the Independence YES/NO question of 2014, and go for an unexpected question this time round?

'Should Scotland be an Independent Country or continue with the process of Brexit?'

That would be a very crafty question indeed. 62% of Scots wanted to stay in the EU in the referendum in 2016, and there was no sign that this percentage had declined at all. Brexit had been handled like a complete dog's breakfast by Westminster, with Scotland (and Wales) side-lined in the whole process.

And such a question would also adhere to Nicola Sturgeon's previous promise not to re-visit the Indy question unless there was, 'a material change of circumstances.' Brexit fitted the bill perfectly.

But, there were also signs that Westminster was secretly planning a new approach to deal with their Scottish problem in the immediate wake of Brexit. At the start of October, a new 'Act of Union' bill was introduced in the House of Lords, designed to re-design and reinforce the 'union' between England, Scotland, Wales and Northern Ireland. Apparently, this new act would herald a new federal arrangement for the four countries. With Mother England still in control of her brood, of course. There was even talk that this idea would be voted upon in a referendum in all four countries post-Brexit. There were clear advantages for Westminster with this idea. For a start, they could control the question and the narrative, rather than letting the SNP do that. It would be their referendum rather than the SNP's. Rather than re-hashing the 'Project Fear' which had been successful in the first referendum in 2104, but which failed so spectacularly in the EU Referendum in 2016 they could this time seek to run a more positive campaign in favour of their 'new union' perhaps. Talk about getting your retaliation in first!

The complexities of the Scotland situation was explained first hand to me and other members of YES Caernarfon at the end of the month. We had been able to persuade one of Scotland's foremost bloggers, Wee Ginger Dug (Paul Kavanagh) to travel down from Glasgow to talk to us.

Scotland is doing a lot of the heavy lifting for us in Wales, in taking on the whole might of the British state and its propaganda outlets. Apparently, 98% of all the mainstream Press and media in Scotland are virulently anti-independence, with this rhetoric stepped up considerably over the past 18 months. A concerted and co-ordinated campaign to destroy the independence cause was at work in Scotland, with resources and direction provided for the 'Scottish media' from elsewhere. We often complain about the dire state of our media here in Wales and the huge information deficit in place here because of that. But if Scotland is an example of what a home-based media can do, perhaps we are better off without for the time being at least. Despite this barrage of negative propaganda, the independence cause is holding up amazingly well as all the latest polls seem to indicate. There's a huge amount we can learn from the whole Scottish experience.

The Castell tavern was packed to hear Wee Ginger Dug, who was accompanied by the famous Dug itself. Paul Kavanagh said the next referendum was not very far away. He also suggested that the sexual harassment allegations against former Scottish First Minister, Alex Salmond, was a clear sign that the decks were being cleared for some form of contest or other over the next few months.

Salmond was preparing to play a big role in the Second Independence Referendum, and these allegations - going back four years - seemed to scupper this leadership role, with a potential court case hanging over him.

But, Salmond, always the gambler, was taking the initiative by taking a case against the Scottish Government to the Court of Sessions concerning the way they had dealt with the matter. This way, the matter would probably be resolved one way or the other much quicker than waiting for a court case.

It appeared that history was repeating itself here. As in the case of Carl Sargeant, the Welsh AM who hung himself after being accused of sexual harassment, without being informed of the nature of the charges against him, Alex Salmond was also seemingly being strung up for similar offences, without being informed of the exact nature of the accusations made against him.

Was Salmond being deliberately removed from the political action in case another snap general election was called in Westminster? It would appear that Theresa May could not hope to get her 'Brexit-lite' Chequers plan through Parliament – with up to 60 Brexiteers declaring they would block it, although she was now even courting centrist Labour MP's to see whether they would be inclined to support her. By hook or by crook, she seems determined to have her way. Theresa May certainly has got an unwavering belief in herself, despite seeing everything crashing down all around her. Including a sign behind her at last year's Conservative Party Confererence, where she was also offered (and meekly accepted), a P45 handed to her right in the middle of her speech by a professional prankster. But, she just ploughs on, oblivious to it all. She must have that same Rhinoceros hide as Trump, I guess. But, despite her bravado, that real P45 can't be that far away now.

But to add to the complexity of the whole picture, the EU had now dismissed the Chequers Plan as totally unworkable, despite all Theresa May's efforts to keep it alive. As well as introducing another red herring late in the day by saying that the UK could actually have what was called a Canada +++ trade deal.

They were also taking full advantage of another big achilles heel for the Westminster Government - Northern Ireland. Northern Ireland was considered to be an essential component of the UK, but after Brexit it would now have to have a border with a country still in the EU, i.e. Eire. The EU Leaders were using NI as a pawn in their political game of chess with the UK in stating that no trade deal could be agreed until the UK decided what shape that border would take. It seemed that England's history on that troubled isle was catching up with her and forcing a momentous decision which could no longer be fudged any more. The EU, although doing their level best to keep the whole of the UK from leaving, seemed to be moving towards a position where if that had to happen eventually, they would demand their pound of flesh. It could be that Northern Ireland would have to be offered up as a sacrificial lamb so that the EU could keep the whole of Ireland in the EU's Single Market and Customs Union and avoid the need for any border between the north and the south.

At the end of the day, it seems to boil down to this. Westminster can either opt to keep their union together, by bowing to the dictates of a tiny proportion of the electorate in Northern Ireland and allow the tail to wag the dog or they can choose Brexit - what the people of England have voted for. They just can't have both. You truly can't have your pudding and eat it whatever Boris Johnson says.

The EU, obviously well aware of Theresa May's weakness and vulnerability in all these areas were upping the ante, in the expectation that she would be willing to make further compromises. Or more likely, they were hoping that the general sense of chaos, confusion and lack of progress would lead to further public clamour in the UK for a second referendum.

The EU have form on this. Over the years, in various referendums, from Ireland to France to Greece, their line has always been - If you don't vote the right way the first time (i.e. in favour of our empire-building project) then we'll invite you to vote again until you come up with the right answer.

Theresa May tried to invoke the spirit of Churchill the next day, wrapping herself in the Union Jack and lashing out at the EU for its 'intransigence' and lack of flexibility. But it was more of a 'Carry On' show than a Churchill display with May almost comical in her protestations about a lady and a proud nation wronged.

The Suez crisis of 1954 was a seminal moment in the 20th Century as it signalled the end of the British Empire in the modern age. Now the Salzburg summit of 2018 seemed to signal the end of British Exceptionalism on the European stage as well. Something had to give.

True to form, there were renewed calls for another referendum, cynically called by another name altogether this time by its proponents, 'the people's vote'.

When the result of one popular referendum just two years previously had just not been truly heeded, and its clarion call for a fundamental change of direction not properly pursued by those in the corridors of power, to call for another referendum on the basis that people were 'misinformed' first time round just seems complete lunacy to me. So people would now be 'informed' this time by these campaigners would they? Right! The proponents of this plan also conveniently forget that both major parties fought a general election last year with manifesto promises to leave both the Single Market and the Customs Union - a position subsequently backed by some 80% of voters. People really don't like parties who break manifesto promises. They really don't. The public also needed another referendum on this matter right now like a hole in the head bearing in mind the division, hostility and raw emotionalism that marked the first.

Such a move would also surely lead to an irrevocable breakdown in the relationship between the rulers and the ruled on these isles. The first Brexit vote was all about a complete lack of trust in the political establishment both in the UK and the EU. Forcing a second vote when the first vote had not been heeded would only make all this ten times worse....

Could another election therefore be way to break the log jam - to see if a new Parliament can be formed with a clear direction of travel as to the UK's future relationship with the EU? Everyone seems to be gearing up for such an election in the Autumn. But then, even that potential scenario seems as clear as mud. Jeremy Corbyn, who sees himself as a Prime Minister in waiting, leads a Labour party which is a complete shambles, with probably the weakest opposition front bench in place for a generation or more. About one hundred Labour MP's are opposed to their own leader and actively plotting a new centrist party.

Corbyn himself also seems blissfully unaware of how unpopular he is as leader, with one recent poll showing that 64 per cent of voters dislike him. That's an even higher dislike factor than achieved by previous leaders Ed Milliband and Gordon Brown, both of whom were deeply distrusted by the voters for various reasons. Some achievement.

At their party conference at Liverpool in September, Keir Starmer seemed to make his own pitch for the leadership, publicly contradicting Corbyn's position on a possible second EU referendum. One section of the party was preparing to vote against Theresa May's chequers deal in order to bring the government down and force a general election. But there was now another section of the party wanting to keep Theresa May in place as Prime Minister by voting for her deal in Parliament. And prevent their own leader from having any chance to gain political power. Big Gee's infamous description of Plaid Cymru as a schizophrenic party was probably even more true of the present Labour party. It's just a complete car wreck all round.

In the meantime, as the equally divided Conservative Party weigh up their own options, there are apparently up to six Tory MP's preparing short and sharp leadership campaigns when PM May is finally put out of her misery. Boris Johnson is one obvious contestant. Despite all his many faults, he would surely be able to provide a clearer Post-Brexit vision than has been provided this past two years, as well as tap into a public mood keen for all the drift and uncertainty to come to an end.

But, despite his popularity with grassroot Tory members, he is also actively despised by many Tory MP's at Westminster, who have already gone on record to say they will do all within their power to prevent him from becoming PM. Someone else could yet steal a march on Boris Johnson.

The two main parties just seem hollowed-out shells by now. Having adopted the same Metropolitan Liberal outlook on life over the past generation, both Labour and the Conservatives now seem a million miles away from their traditional supporters. Their respective party conferences in September have the appearance of a complete charade and look to be increasingly archaic and ridiculous concepts to most of the public by now, propped up only by a mainstream media desperate to keep the whole show on the road....

There's just no way of knowing how all this will pan out. All the normal rules of engagement both within the established political parties and between them and the electorate in general all seem to have been suspended entirely for the foreseeable future. It's just unchartered territory for all concerned, Expect the unexpected as they say.

We seem passive and helpless onlookers in Wales as all these political games are going on all around us, in England, in Scotland, and with the EU. But, it could all come in handy one day.

Yes, all we've been doing is watching and listening as other people in other places do all the running. But there's also some deep learning going on in the wake of all the recent important developments on these isles over the years.

All this observation, all this information, all this learning will be invaluable as we face the future and make our own decisions in due course.

PEN PORTRAIT 11:

Phil Roberts.
Born Chester. Living in Nant Bwlch Yr Haearn, Betws Y Coed

I have previously not had much of an interest in politics so why have I decided now to become involved with Ein Gwlad?

That is a big question, so firstly I had to assess why my previous lack of interest? The main reason I have concluded is that all the established political parties have a pre-ordained dogma which therefore lacks flexibility. The political environment is such that you have to 'buy into' all of the constitution of a party or reject it altogether. Where is the sense in this?

Circumstances change and therefore the solutions to problems may also change and when politics becomes this rigid to my mind it is unworkable. For years Wales as a country has been side-lined and ignored by both the London based government and the other political parties. Our assembly government does not seem to stand up for the Welsh people and the Welsh nation rarely warrants a mention in the news, weather or any viable public media and this has become an increasing frustration

Ein Gwlad offers a fresh approach to politics as it aims to be a syncretic party and is therefore not afraid of taking ideas from across the political spectrum. It is not bound to a particular set of rules and ideas and this is an exciting and really revolutionary way of approaching politics.

The fact therefore that Ein Gwlad is inclusive and will aim to embrace any ideas and opportunities has made me interested in the party. Involving people from any side of the political spectrum with the aim of improving the life of the Welsh people is something worth fighting to achieve so that we can give our children a better future

August 28th 2018

Launch day of Ein Gwlad, Samuel Centre, Llanelli, Carmarthenshire.

The long and tricky road to any kind of political influence in Wales lies ahead. So indeed no doubt, will be the fall-outs, the cock-ups, the personality clashes, the frustrations, the in-fighting and the jostling for personal status and power and the sheer fatigue that eventually paralyses and cripples all political parties. Think the Labour Party. The Conservative Party. And here in Wales, think Plaid Cymru.

But today has been a special day. After all, months of hard work have led to this moment. Despite all the wrong turns, the misunderstandings, the resignations, the frustrations and the doubts, Ein Gwlad is now out there in the public arena.

We don't have to worry about the challenges of tomorrow. Everybody present here today can just enjoy the event. This moment. This experience. This triumph.

I guess today's been kind of redemptive for me on a personal level.

But today's been much more important and significant than that.

Twenty-five registered supporters turned up to hear the Chairperson of Ein Gwlad, Gwilym ab Ioan announce the arrival of a new political party for Wales dedicated to the cause of independence.

They have also been introduced to the concept that Ein Gwlad will be a syncretic party, willing to consider and develop policies from all directions if those policies will benefit Wales as a country.

This party will not be sustaining the tired and old-fashioned left-right axis. But neither will it be aiming for the safe and tepid centre.

Wales has to be transformed and now it has a transformational party willing to undertake that work in the years ahead.

Welsh and English interviews were conducted with our spokespersons, Gwyn Wigley Evans and Stephen Morris. Both were clear, decisive and persuasive in their answers. And humorous as well!

The five main question asked at the launch:

What do you hope to achieve in launching Ein Gwlad?

In a word, Independence. The reason for that is that we want to see living standards in Wales improve. A century of being dominated by the Labour Party has left Wales as one of the poorest countries in Europe, and yet all over the world, there are successful independent countries as small as Wales but with much higher living standards. We Want Wales to become one of them.

How will you promote Ein Gwlad?

By not being boring. Political discussion in this country has become stultified to the point hardly anyone ever says something unexpected, and political correctness has put many subjects effectively off–limits. We will engage with people where they are, on social media, by word of mouth and talk about the things that really matter to people. We think that means being able to live their lives with dignity, being treated fairly and with respect and being supported in making
their lives better for themselves and their communities.

You say you are a syncretic party. The first of its kind in Britain. What does that actually mean?

We are not left-wing nor are we right-wing and we are definitely not centrist.
We'll take ideas from anywhere, so long as they'll work for Wales. I'll give you an example. We support the idea of a citizens' income which many would consider a left-wing policy. We also advocate a flat tax rate, which many would say is a policy of the right. We believe that if you put the two together, what you get is not a compromise, but rather a powerful argument to boost the economy, encourage enterprise and ensure genuine fairness at all levels of society.

The mainstream press and media were not invited to the launch. Why was that?

Very simply, we do not believe in the group-think and politically correct paralysis that afflicts most of the legacy media in Wales and beyond. We don't think they have the capacity to understand what we are about, let alone report

on us accurately. We would much rather engage with the Welsh
people directly, on their terms and ours.

Do you think you will have elected representatives in place at Y Senedd in 2021?

We believe there is a huge pent-up demand in Wales for a party that can provide a realistic alternative to Labour with radically different policies and yet without the baggage and distrust which dogs all the other parties in Wales. We believe we have the arguments and the integrity to offer that alternative and we'd be astonished if that didn't translate into a significant share of the vote.

The Answers to those five key questions about Ein Gwlad have been pared down to twenty seconds in Welsh and twenty seconds in English: it will add up to a three-minute film to go out on social media tonight. Three minutes apparently is the golden rule concerning the internet in today's media saturated world. Any more than that, and you lose people's attention. Gwyn has done his homework.

Another ten questions and answers about Ein Gwlad have been recorded and these will be released gradually on social media over the next few weeks to build up momentum.

The supporters at the launch were engaged and enthused and took part in a filmed section to explaining why they have joined Ein Gwlad themselves.

These clips will also be released on social media over the same timescale. After all, people buy people.

And more than anything else, a confident tone of ambition was present throughout the proceedings, and a route map to a possible share of power outlined to the supporters as well. It was great to see a combination of Welsh speakers and English speakers present, with everyone mixing together and getting on with each other so well. Sian Caiach, our latest recruit to the Steering Committee tells Gwyn later that this sense of togetherness was one of the main stand-out features of the day for her.

Gwyn drives me to the station in Llanelli to get the train back home. I sit back on the train with a huge sense of relief. Job done. For the time being at least. And now, I've got two weeks off. I'm going travelling in Vietnam for a fortnight!

Thoughts of Steering Committee Members at the launch:

Mike Murphy:
'It has been an interesting few months to say the least, starting with interminable discussions about the party name and logo and finishing with a mad scramble of activity leading up to the launch. In between, we have had some fascinating discussions about different from the politics as usual from the established parties. Ein Gwlad was set up to system of pigeon-holing people into political categories like left, right, centre, whatever it is. Ein Gwlad doesn't discriminate and uses ideas from across the whole political spectrum for the betterment of the lives of everyone in Wales."

Stephen Morris:
'Today, more than any other time, I feel "this is real"- we're really doing this, and we're not just sounding off on social media or setting the world to rights in the pub. We're doing this for real, and it's going to change things. Are we ready?
My hope is that we can maintain our focus and our discipline. We've poked a stick into more than one nest of very grumpy hornets and we are now going to see the other side's dark arts deployed against us. We need to keep our nerve and never lose sight of the fact that we are doing this for Wales."

Dennis Morris:
'Although it has only been ten or so months since we first got together, it seems longer. The enthusiasm displayed by those involved in setting up the party has been incredible. Today is a dawn for Welsh Politics. Ein Gwlad will bring new ideas into the political arena, concepts that will be for the benefit of Cymru and its citizens. How refreshing is that.
My aspiration for Ein Gwlad is that it will be seen as the true guardians of our nation and a party that will grow in strength

and regarded as authentic and uncompromising in its quest for an independent state of Cymru. We have exciting times ahead of us and I'm very happy to be on board.'

James Llewelyn-Henton:

'The Launch today was a great success in my view. Those of our supporters that came were able to engage with us and find out all that they wanted to know and more. One of our supporters before he left even said how he has always been apolitical, but now he believes he's found something he can truly get behind, which for me is a great thing to see because it is clear we are what many people in Cymru have been desperately waiting for.

What I see for us now is to build on our success here spreading the word to every corner of Cymru about what we hope for this magnificent little nation we proudly call home. There are clearly a great many people who want something different, so now is our time to work with communities all over Cymru, so that we can show the people who is willing to do this for their future, every step of the way to make this nation prosper.

We will no doubt have a lot of hard work ahead of us in the run-up to the 2021 elections for the Senedd, but I'm sure any obstacles in our way will fall swiftly, especially as we're the only party with an ideology that can accommodate all that call our nation home.'

Gwyn Wigley Evans:

'A sense of amazement at the amount of work it takes to launch a political party properly and the surprise that we have such a dedicated group of diverse talents that work together so well. Without that, it could not have happened. The numbers that turned up and their unqualified enthusiasm was a major shot in the arm. I am also aware looking at the wider political field in Wales and the UK, how timely this whole event has been. Not only is there a need, but the public are looking and questioning some very fundamental positions and may be willing to move from their traditional homes.'

'With my selling hat on that I've worn and battered over the last fifty years, we established there was a 'need'. This is one of the first principles of marketing. Selling is turning that 'need' into a 'want'. That is our huge task against all the forces of the establishment. We are seeing the attention on social media already, but that's a compliment. I would be more worried if there was silence.

Lee Felton:
'At the launch, I felt excited as I hadn't been involved in helping to set up a new political party before. It's a new experience I feel fortunate to have been part of. I'm fairly new to the party and have only been involved a few months. I help with the graphics side of things and administer the Facebook page.

Going forward, I hope to see the party grow its membership. I think this will take time because we don't rely so much on the mainstream media. But, I genuinely believe that Ein Gwlad can make an impact on the political stage in Wales. People here are crying out for something of our vision and policies, and I am certain we have ended up with the right outcome.

Even before the launch, we have been noticed by the other parties who are reacting to our statements. I expect their reactions to increase in strength and frequency which means we will have achieved one of our main objectives-to shake up Welsh politics. The next step is to win power and seats in the Senedd and I expect that we will have a significant presence after 2021 and we will use that presence to change Wales for the better.

PEN PORTRAIT 12

Aled Gwyn Jôb:
Born Llanelwy. Living in Caernarfon.

So then, what do I bring to the party? There are more eloquent and cleverer people than myself all around me in this enterprise. But then, as the old saying goes, if you are not in a room with smarter people than yourself, you are in the wrong room.

Apart from my writing, I like to think that I bring a certain amount of determination to the process. As my father always loves to point out to people who harp on about the "patience of Job", the Biblical Job was not known for his patience, but rather his perseverance. And wasn't there also an infamous Soviet leader who once said that history is made by those who turn up?

I would also like to think that I have a certain fearlessness about me which is somehow hard to define. It seems an odd quality for an Introvert to lay claim to, but perhaps faith does that to you. When you trust in God's sustenance and his provisions for you in life, you no longer need or fear the opinions and approval of those around you. There's great power in Henry David Thoreaux's words· himself a great walker· "Above Love, above Wealth, above Fame·give me Truth".

And of course there's "And you shall seek for the truth and the truth shall set you free". There's a longing inside me for truth. That's my reason for committing to Ein Gwlad - to tell people the truth about Wales's situation, to be truthful with people about what needs to be done to improve our country and be truthful in all our subsequent dealings with the people of Wales.

And I genuinely think other people are thirsting for truth as well. People of all ages are fed-up with all the lies, the spin, manipulation, self-interest, arrogance, pomposity and sheer greed of the political class in Wales and elsewhere. I think we could be pushing at an open door with a new dedication to the truth.

I believe Ein Gwlad can also provide our nation with a completely different way of doing politics. Away with the old mantra: "We the politicians know best"- to a more participative, bottom-up model where everyone of all ages can contribute to new political, social and economic answers for Wales. Let's build the most participative and people-centred democracy in Europe.

And I hope there's also an audience in Wales for a more libertarian approach to politics for a clean break from the dead hand of top-down and statist Labour/Plaid rule over the devolution period in Wales. Where we trust people to be able to be more responsible for their own decisions and allow people more freedom in every aspect of their lives.

I genuinely think Wales could be the best small country in the world to live in. But we need Independence first.

So what happens next?

After the launch, Ein Gwlad will prepare for its first Annual National Conference to be held in Newtown early next year. At that event, the Steering Committee will be wound up, and new officers will be elected on behalf of the party. The first raft of policies will be drawn up in preparation for the next Assembly Elections of 2021.

The main target will be to win regional seats at that election. The National Assembly is composed of sixty members. Forty of these are chosen on a constituency basis, but twenty are chosen on a proportional representation basis to properly reflect the cast votes nationwide. Four members are chosen in this way in five regions: north wales, mid and west wales, south west wales, south wales central, south east central.

Policy Co-ordinator Mike Murphy has worked out that 5% of the regional vote would lead to one representative for Ein Gwlad at the next Assembly after those Elections. The way the system works, 10% of the vote would mean five or six members. He thinks that is a realistic target to aim for.

There are three years to go before all that. Nobody knows of course, how things will pan out over that space of time, nor whether the party can gain any traction amongst the voting public in Wales.

But, the call for change all round will be a clear theme by 2021, and that will be a definite plus for a brand-new party standing at those elections for the very first time.

With the whole of Wales knowing that the end of Labour Party rule is well overdue, it's not completely inconceivable that there could be some form of alternative coalition formed for the new 2021 term, featuring the Conservatives, Plaid Cymru and Ein Gwlad to govern Wales. Who knows, YES Cymru could even join the party!

It really would be a whole new political dawn for Wales. Would Plaid Cymru finally abandon their ideological opposition to the hated Tories to be part of such a coalition and for an opportunity to seek to transform the political fortunes of Wales. And consign Welsh Labour to the dustbin of history in the bargain?

All that will depend entirely on the result of the Plaid Cymru leadership contest which culminates at the end of September. It's more than likely that both Rhun ap Iorwerth and Adam Price would be willing sign up to such a coalition in some shape or form.

But, it's hard to see Leanne Wood abandoning her lifelong opposition to the Conservatives both in London and in Wales, having made it such a make-or-break issue for her personally.

Another big plus for her in the contest is that she's got an influential coalition whom I would term the 'Pragmatic Plaidies' on her side. These people believe that, on balance, it's safer for Plaid to continue with Leanne at the helm. There is a concern, afraid that if Leanne loses - her leftist orientated supporters would throw their toys out of the pram and make things very, very difficult for the winner.

They believe there could be a further period of dissension and conflict to follow which could make the disagreements and fall-outs of the past year appear like a Sunday School tea party in comparison.

However, when the result is finally announced at the end of September, the 'Pragmatic Plaidies' argument falls on stony ground. Adam Price wins by a clear margin, gaining 49.7% of the votes in the first round, with Rhun ap Iorwerth in second place with 28% of the vote. Leanne Wood polls a shockingly poor 22%. All that high visibility in the campaign and all those declarations of support for her on social media ultimately proved to be a complete illusion. ITV's Political Editor, Adrian Masters, reveals that five hundred SNP members from Scotland actually joined Plaid Cymru during the contest to vote en-bloc for Leanne Wood. That means that her figures were even more dire than would appear at first glance.

An even more startling fact is that 30% of the Plaid Cymru membership did not bother to vote at all! In a vote which was touted as the most important one to be held by the party in two generations.

Adam Price seems set for a honeymoon period as new leader. Many of the members seem uplifted and galvanised by his victory, and he certainly puts his oratorical and assertive skills to work almost immediately saying that a 'No Deal' Brexit would lead to Welsh Independence.

"He's talked more about Independence in one weekend than Leanne Wood did for six years," said one enthusiastic member to

me after his victory. Mind you, Adam Price hedged his bets at the same time by saying that Plaid Cymru would also support the call for a 'People's Vote' on the final deal thrashed out with Brussels.

Plaid members might well have voted overwhelmingly for change, but how much change would it prove to be be in truth, once the honeymoon is over? On a radio programme just before the vote, all three candidates were asked to describe themselves in one word. Rhun ap Iorwerth said "nationalist". Leanne Wood and Adam Price both said "socialist". Plaid members may have just squeezed out the nationalist and swapped one socialist for another one. Still wedded to Welsh Labour and business as usual down in Cardiff Bay.

Mike Murphy puts up an article on the Ein Gwlad website with the title:

'All change at the top, but how much of a change is it really?' highlighting the continuation from the Leanne Wood regime, not only because of the joint socialist leanings, but also in view of the fact that Adam Price was Leanne Wood's political guru and speech-writer for the past six years.

Stephen Morris weighs in with another hefty article on nation.cymru making the same point about business as usual in the bay, and the need for a different approach. He also flags one key area where Ein Gwlad will pursue a very different course to Plaid.

'Ein Gwlad will also stand fearlessly for freedom, not only national freedom but individual freedom, away from the statist and top-down thinking which so dominates Plaid/Labour's world view. That will include a renewed commitment to free speech and the right of people to express their opinions openly, without being shut down by a 'thought police' mentality. Let all schools of thought

contend with each other openly in Wales and may the best one win,' he writes.

With such clear differences now being outlined between the two parties, perhaps it's not such a bad result for Ein Gwlad after all…

An Independence Referendum?

As for any future independence referendum for Wales, newly elected Plaid Cymru leader Adam Price recently suggested it should be held in 2030, following two Plaid Cymru terms in government in Cardiff Bay. That seems a very long time away. I sense it could happen much before that.

At the start of October, a new opinion poll puts support for Welsh Independence at 19%, up from 7% just a year ago. That's the highest recorded figure I can ever remember. The tectonic plates are most certainly starting to shift in wake of all the political turmoil of the last two years.

If Scotland votes for independence - and that new vote seems likely to happen either next year or 2020 - that changes everything. Wales could then face a Serbia/Montenegro situation.

When the old Yugoslavia broke up in 1996, four of the different constituent parts went their own way, including Slovenia, and Croatia. That then left Serbia with little old Montenegro, with only its 600,000 strong population left of the old Yugoslavia.

Nobody thought that Montenegro would ever want to break away from Serbia after its long historical and religious connection with Serbia, and after being overshadowed by its bigger neighbour for so many centuries.

Despite being a country with a national history stretching back to the 9th century, the people of Montenegro had always seemed uncertain and wary of any talk of independence. On top of that, 32% of their population was actually Serbian, who saw no difference between Serbia and Montenegro and therefore opposed independence from the start.

In the run-up to the Independence referendum which eventually occurred in May 2006, the Serbian Government also campaigned openly against the prospect of their small neighbour going its own way. They even called it a 'stab in the back'.

But in the referendum itself on an 86% turn-out, 55.5% of the population of Montenegro voted for Independence - just clearing the 55% threshold that had been agreed. Montenegro became an internationally recognised independent country.

For Montenegro and Serbia, read Wales and England. And there are other similarities that could be drawn between Montenegro and Wales.

Montenegro has a sea coast and has stunning geography with dramatic mountain ranges.

It's marketing itself as 'one of the most beautiful countries in Europe'. They are also investing in transforming Montenegro into a country of 'ideas, information and knowledge.' They could easily have lifted those definitions from Wales itself.

I can see the Montenegro option arriving a lot quicker than anyone anticipates. At that point, the people of Wales will have the choice between staying part of Greater England after Scotland votes for Independence or they can follow the example of the people of Montenegro and decide upon their own national future.

Having voted to establish the Welsh Assembly by a narrow margin in 1999, and then voting to increase the Assembly's powers in much greater numbers back in 2011, the ground has already been laid for that third decisive vote, a vote for Independence.

I'm confident that when push comes to shove, the people of Wales will be persuaded by the Montenegro Precedent.

Hopefully, by the time that referendum finally arrives, the people of Wales will have been informed, encouraged and inspired by the arrival of an out-and-out Independence party. A party assisted in that task by a movement organising and mobilising towards that goal throughout civic society in Wales, in the shape of YES Cymru. And if Adam Price sustains his early and promising rhetoric as party leader, Plaid Cymru will also be fully on board the independence train.

Hopefully all involved will also have learnt important lessons in the wake of all the rancour, division and recriminations over the past two years following the EU vote. The public quite simply are fed-up to the back teeth with all this negativity, point scoring and public falling-out within parties and between parties. Unity of purpose and spirit between all concerned will have to be in place from the very start in any Independence campaign.

Big Gee expresses this need for a new consensus in Wales with his trademark perception and eloquence on the forum:

"We may squabble about our internal politics in Cymru - fine, but when it comes to our freedom, we have to be as one. It's a bit like having family arguments. Families can argue and fall out, but if someone from next door gets involved, the family stands together as one. Plaid are 'family' at the end of the day - we may not see eye-to-eye on everything, but family is family."

And when that independence referendum finally arrives, perhaps we could derive inspiration from the 'rebel manifesto' drawn up by some of the campaigners who fought a David and Goliath battle against the establishment in the European referendum of 2016, to deliver the biggest shock to the political system for a century.

As Sebastian Handley puts it in his book "Brexit- How the Nobodies beat the Somebodies"

"They said the experts knew best- but we doubted their sincerity and impartiality

"They said "Listen"- we said, "Look"

They beat us in the gated media - we did better on social media

They said "Don't Change"- we said "Change"

They said "Be Scared"- we said "Don't Be Scared"

They had leaders- we had an idea"

So, what can other would-be political hopefuls learn from our experience this past year? What are the lessons and tips we can pass on to any others thinking of starting up new political parties in this post-Brexit landscape, where all the established parties seem so washed out, so discredited, so unpopular?

The new Back Together party, rumoured to be starting up in the new year with their millions in the bank and New Labour influences won't need any help or suggestions in that direction, that's for sure. But, for anyone else, who's encouraged to have a go, maybe you need three core components. A vision to inspire you, a leader to motivate you and a commitment to sustain you. If you can conjure up those three essential features and keep those equally in place as you journey towards forming a new party, you've got a decent chance.

I would urge people to go for it. There's nothing quite like political activism. It's fantastic for your mental and emotional health to involve yourself in something which is beyond your own day-to-day personal existence.

And there's nothing quite like working together with other like-minded people to work towards a noble objective. That objective might well appear impossible and completely out of reach at times. But that just makes the joint striving, dreaming, planning and discussing to try and achieve it, that much more special and meaningful.

It's a fantastic way to make new friends. And create deep and lasting bonds with those people. There's an additional charge to political activism which makes it much stronger than other forms of community involvement where people come together to partake in different activities.

Being part of a gardening club or involvement with a community choir or a literary society all provide their own benefits for people of course, but there's something about trying to change society, to change a country, to change the very course of its history, which goes way beyond those particular benefits.

I would go as far to say that political activism could be the perfect antidote for the alienation, loneliness and general unhappiness that seems to characterise modern society, not only in Wales but in the rest of these isles as well. What better way to tackle these three huge modern evils than engage in political activity with other people to improve your own life and improve the life of the society around you? It's liberating. It's empowering. It's life itself.

When it comes to society, there's been a lot of talk recently about a crisis of masculinity in our modern world. And no doubt, there's a lot of truth in all this. The fact that 90% of homeless people and 82% of prisoners in the UK are male is maybe just the tip of the iceberg. Three times more men than women commit suicide every year.

There's a sense that the loss of traditional industries over the past two generations has led to some form of a crisis of identity for men in modern society. What exactly are we for, now that our roles have changed so much over the past few years? Many men seem so dispensable in so many ways today somehow.

This year of course we've also heard about all the sexual accusations against a Hollywood mogul who has most likely misused his power over women actresses for many years. And there's the never-ending scandal of child abuse perpetrated by male Catholic Clergy all over the world. We all seem to be implicated in all this somehow.

There have been two further hideous revelations of church abuse in Ireland and America these past few months. The Pope, on an official visit to Ireland, has just been accused by an Archbishop of covering up for a known child abuser in America. All this seems to be never ending. It's grim being a man today.

But what I've found over this past year is that it's not all bad news for men. I'm sure that Phil (Phillipa) - our national treasurer, and Sian Caiach our newest addition to the steering committee - won't mind me saying that the process of establishing Ein Gwlad has been a predominantly male affair.

For me, this year has been a demonstration of the worth of what could be termed traditional male values: Courage, Persistence, Leadership, Focus, Nerve and Sheer Bloody-Mindedness.

Those qualities have been found in spades amongst the Steering Committee these past few months with Gwilym setting the tone for it all with his absolute dedication to the cause, despite not being in the best of health personally. He's led by example by putting in one hell of a shift. What can I say about Big Gee? He's just a force of nature. He's truly been inspirational.

I feel honoured to have worked alongside these guys and gal(!) for the past year. I've become a better person, a more complete person through all this. I've also learnt a huge amount just by being in their company and plugging into some really fertile and creative minds. It's been like another Aberystwyth University experience for me. But one that's been much richer and much more fulfilling this time round.

And achieved in the company of other middle-aged wrinklies as well. James excepted of course! Middle age doesn't have to be such a dead end after all. It can be a place of new dreams, new hopes, new ambitions and new horizons.

The younger generation just don't know what they are missing. If they could just get off their phones, forget about social media and consumerism for a while, they could find life waiting patiently for them to get on board. In the meantime, I suppose us middle-agers have got to continue to put them to shame. And continue to flourish by doing so.

The friendship and understanding that has blossomed between us, the fierce camaraderie forged by these months of effort, our loyalty to each other and our vision, and the egalitarian ethos of the whole project somehow seems to provide a metaphor for the kind of independent country we hope to see.

A country which is faithful to its roots. A country which has a noble vision of itself and its place in the world. A country based on connection and loyalty between people. A country where everyone matters.

The whole project seems by now to be much more than just a process of starting up a new political party. It feels more like a mission. A crusade. It feels more like…it feels more like…. revival.

Wales has been a land marked by religious revivals over the past few centuries, and even now, as secular as modern Wales undoubtedly is, you can't get away from those underlying currents. The last Welsh revival took place in 1904. Some have been saying for a while that another one is long overdue.

But what if this time it's a different type of revival altogether? Not the power of the pulpit this time, but the power of the people. The power of the people to revive Wales in every way.

Despite my background, I'm not the biggest fan of organised religion, to be totally honest. But faith is a different. After all, faith can move mountains.

The legendary American soul singer Aretha Franklin has just died. I watch some of the epic seven-hour funeral on television. One of my all-time favourite songs of hers, 'People Get Ready' is played. That amazing voice, full of spirit, grace and power rings out again. From across the Atlantic, the words seem to resonate with Wales's situation today:

> People get ready, there's a train coming,
> Don't need no ticket, we'll just get on board
> All you need is faith to hear that diesel humming…

The very name, Ein Gwlad should also be a metaphor for a more wide-ranging process which goes way beyond an individual political entity. It should be an invitation to something more creative and inspirational than conventional politicking, which is so off-putting for most normal people. It should seek to engender that sense of fun, friendliness, togetherness, spirit, engagement and good-will that a good party always encourages amongst people. The people of Wales really deserve a good party after all we've been through over the years. Hopefully Plaid Cymru, Ein Gwlad and Yes Cymru can all create that party atmosphere here over the next few years. Perhaps Wales could follow Scotland's example again and set up a National Independence Convention consisting of all the different parties and groups in favour of Independence and create one united front to present the message to the people of Wales.

Nearing my mid-fifties, I'm highly unlikely to become a father again which is a shame because fatherhood has probably been the best thing that has ever happened in my life, and I sometimes feel a yearning for it again.

But somehow, I feel that I myself have given birth to a new creation this past year through writing about the formation of

Ein Gwlad and the future for ein gwlad(our nation) as a whole. As the words have flowed, so has the tide flowed in the direction of a new start for Wales.

Now though, I am all set to write a brand-new chapter in my own life. The walk goes on, the path continues, and another University experience awaits. I'm going to study Theology and Society at Cardiff.

Who knows, perhaps this development tells me that it's time to walk away from the party that I've played a part in creating this past year.

In a way, I've already mentally detached myself from the process that takes place after officially launching the party anyway. Ein Gwlad might be a complete flop. We don't know. But that doesn't matter really.

What I do know is that Independence for Wales is a historically inevitable event. It will happen. In my lifetime.

That idea - that vision - is more important than any one single party, and even if Ein Gwlad achieves no electoral success as such, we've furthered the cause of independence by presenting it into the political mainstream in Wales, at long last.

I, like Wales have been at a low point in my existence. Everything looked hopeless. Everything looked bleak.

But, I've recovered and created a new future for myself. So can Wales.

Author walking in the Peak District over Christmas.
Big D lurking in the background as ever

Doting Father (the Author) and Daughter soon to fly away to university

A Bright New Dawn for Wales - On the prom at Aberystwyth.

The Free Traws Cymru bus on Saturday.
This has proved so popular since its inception

The Phoenix chosen as the logo for the new party.

EIN GWLAD
Not left, not right- just Welsh

Home   About Ein Gwlad   Ein Gwlad Branches   Our Constitution   Our Aims and Principles   Membership   ↓

Volunteer   Donations   Political News (Wales)   Ein Gwlad's Blog   Contact Ein Gwlad

Steering Committee at work at Canolfan y Morlan, Aberystwyth.
From left to right, Lee, James, Aled, Gwilym, Phil, Dennis, Sian, Gwyn

Ein Gwlad logo: 'Not left, not right, just Welsh'

Supporters who gathered together at the launch, Canolfan Samuel, Llanelli, August 28, 2018

Wee Ginger Dug with Yes Caernarfon officers: Gwion Hallam, Gwion Owain, Aled Gwyn Job

Wee Ginger Dug (Paul Kavanagh) addressing a packed meeting
at Y Castell, Caernarfon

Dr. Stephen Morris, Gwilym ab Ioan and Gwyn Wigley Evans at the launch

Gwyn Wigley Evans, Interim Leader, talking at the launch

Svetana and Dale outside their Dome cafe, Bangor, Gwynedd.

Ein Gwlad on tour in Vietnam- the Land of the Phoenix

A top of the mountain experience on the road to Lang Co, Vietnam.

Eating a local delicacy along the Mekong Delta : shredded snake with herbs and crispy veg. Big D says it's good practice for all the snakes in the grass of Welsh politics!

Sapa, Vietnam gives Wales a good run for its money in the natural beauty stakes.